OUR SECRET RHYTHM

OUR SECRET RHYTHM

The Vibrational Universal Connection

By
Bill Carmichael

ISBN (eBook/Kindle): 979-8-218778-22-4

ISBN (Paperback): 978-1-968012-39-7

ISBN (Hardcover): 978-1-968012-40-3

Library Of Congress Catalog Card Number:

Published in the United States of America by Lynx Publishers.

DEDICATION

Thank you to my wife Wendy for her love and
patience during my creative process.

CONTENTS

INTRODUCTION

What if every breath you have ever taken, every thought that has flickered across your mind, and every sound that has reached your ears was never random, but instead a note in a far greater composition? What if your very heartbeat is but one instrument playing within an eternal symphony—subtle, unseen, and yet profoundly real?

This book, *Our Secret Rhythm*, is the story of my journey into that awareness. It is not a theory, nor a philosophy detached from life, but a living account of how ordinary moments—some joyous, others marked by deep struggle—revealed themselves as doorways into a vibrational universal rhythm that connects us all.

For much of my life, I have found myself immersed in a world of vibrational energies. I learned to listen differently— beyond the surface of noise and into the hidden currents that shape both harmony and dissonance. Through this work, which outwardly seemed ordinary yet quietly opened extraordinary doors, I began to sense that life itself is tuned by forces beyond sight or measurement.

In these pages, you will find not only my story, but reflections of your own. For though our paths are different, the vibrational rhythm we are part of is the same. You may find comfort here, or inspiration, or even answers to questions you did not yet know you were asking.

OUR SECRET RHYTHM

Our Secret Rhythm is not simply a memoir, nor only a guide. It is a conversation—between myself and you, between the past and the present, between the seen and the unseen. It is a reminder that we are never truly alone, and that the symphony of life is always unfolding within and around us.

I invite you to walk with me now into this story. Listen closely. Perhaps you will hear something—faint yet undeniable—that has been with you all along.

1

TRIALL RAIK

From deep within a beautiful, enchanted world that my conscious self—Leith—hoped to reside in, I felt a profound sense of contentment, mixed with a longing so gentle it was almost holy. This realm pulsed with peace. It shimmered like starlight caught in the folds of silk, a sacred space suspended between the known and the unknowable. I felt, for a fleeting moment, as though I had returned to the source of all things.

This was a place that unified all dimensions, where light did not simply illuminate—it became all things. It blended effortlessly into itself, folding into one radiant whole. Boundaries dissolved. There were no edges. No fixed lines. Just an ever-becoming stream of being.

Here, there was no sense in what some would refer to as time. Time, as I had once known it, was a distortion of the physical realm. In this sacred place, there was no past, no present, no future—only what was, what is, and what will always be, flowing together like an eternal river. Everything on this celestial plane existed in a state of perfect and total vibrational harmony. There was no resistance, no friction, only deep coherence—a resonance that echoed through all that existed.

Whether one was arriving from another incarnation, or passing on to another realm, whether they came from the stars, the Earth, or some dimension yet unnamed, there was only one sacred law: to exist in complete and total vibrational harmony with all things. With the stones. With the trees. With the galaxies. With the silent mysteries between breaths.

Yet I knew—somehow, I knew—that my soul's conscious fate had not yet been fully decided. I was still in a state of becoming, not quite settled, not yet anchored. Something still remained unfinished.

Off in the distance, a glowing mist began to gather. It shimmered faintly at first, like dew caught in morning light, then thickened, swelled, and began to move with purpose. Slowly, it approached me, curling around my conscious self, wrapping me in something that felt like memory and prophecy all at once.

From within that mist, the glowing ones emerged. Ethereal and radiant, they moved not with steps but with presence. They were the ancient elders—a tribunal of immense wisdom—and they were the gatekeepers of this eternal world. Their eyes, if they could be called eyes, held all of history, and none. Their voices did not speak but vibrated into the marrow of my soul, bypassing all thought and language.

As I stood before them, weightless and still, they addressed me not with words, but in pure vibrational unison, as one eternal voice of thought. They said, "Leith, your name means flowing water; and so, like the water that flows through you, so too must you flow again upon your journey."

Their decree rang through me. With that, my fate had been sealed. I had not yet earned the right to stay in this sacred place. My time in this realm was not over, but neither was it complete. I was not being punished. I was being reminded. Reminded that even light must move, that even souls must evolve beyond their longing.

I did not want to leave. I ached to remain in that beautiful space, to dissolve into its luminous embrace and become one with the song of the spheres. But I bowed to the will of the elders. I had to respect the decision, for they saw further than I could. They were the keepers of balance, and I still had ripples to send across the water of existence.

They instructed me to return to the path—to unify all the layers of my conscious self into one harmonic vibration. Only then could I return home. Only then would I be ready to enter the stillness I had glimpsed.

Their final words to me were spoken with solemn beauty:

Triall Raik—the ancient Scottish phrase meaning journey forward.

And so, the elders slowly faded back into the glowing mist. Their forms, like lanterns in fog, dissolved into memory. As they vanished, I too began to descend from that luminous world—softly, slowly—into a spiraling, dreamlike state.

I was flowing again, as they said I must. My journey was not yet over.

THE AWAKENING

Slowly there was a sense of awakening- like rising from an ancient slumber long ago. A gentle, almost perfect warmth surrounded me giving me a feeling of perfect calmness and contentment.

Far off in the distance, as if carried like a feather on a distant wind, slowly towards me, I began to sense a familiar sound approaching. It was calm, rhythmic vibration- perfectly timed, like the soft beat of an ancient drum. It was a feeling I knew so well from long ago, and it brought me peace and love. A soothing comforting rhythmic thumping echoed around me.

I heard other familiar vibrations too- subtle squishing and gentle gurgling sounds. Within the perfect darkened capsule, I had a sense of seeing before I could truly see. There was also a gentle swinging motion, like leaves blowing in a soft breeze. They were sensations I knew too well- familiar to me from a distant past.

Suddenly my whole world grew tense. The tremendous vibrations intensified, growing faster and stronger. Once again, something familiar was happening. I was being pushed from comfort into the unknown. Deep down, I knew this forward motion was inevitable. I had no choice but to surrender even if it wasn't what I wanted.

Slowly, a tiny distant light appeared, growing larger as the vibrations around me continued to force me toward it. I had no control-only the pull toward that light. Then, in an instant, I suddenly emerged into an intense cold bright world.

An unwelcoming feeling and a sense of fear came over my helpless body as a sharp stinging feeling struck me from behind. I let out what was my first cry, and as those in the room sighed in relief. I quickly began being shuffled from one set of hands to another until I was placed in the soft familiar warmth-the steady comforting of a thumping heartbeat that I knew by heart.

It was my mother.

As a nuzzled into her warm body, I began to feel a sense of peace and protection again, though my surroundings had greatly changed. She looked down at me, smiled, and said, "welcome my beautiful baby boy, your name shall be Will."

Wrapped tightly in her loving arms, I felt a flicker of joy and anticipation for my life ahead. I was hopeful for the love and guidance of parents waiting to unfold around me.

Like all babies, my early days were filled with frequent feeding, followed by frequently relieving myself and then much-needed sleep. Various sounds surrounded me, creating vibrations and frequencies I could feel but barely understand at my young age. Yet too often, the calm serenity of my surroundings was shattered by loud violent screaming and yelling, causing a completely disruptive atmosphere within my little world.

This was the presence of my biological father.

I could sense his intensely negative vibrational energy. He routinely disrupted and obliterated any peace and calmness in the household, replacing it with fear. The violent yelling between him and my mother was deafening, each word creating negative vibrational energy that coursed through every cell in my tiny body.

This was the man I was supposed to call "Daddy."

Slowly, the nurturing, love and presence of my mother began to fade. The warmth of her breast, the comfort of her embrace, the lullabies she once sang in soft Scottish tones- all of it slipped away. I began to sense others in the home, and from some ancient place of knowing, I recognized them as my siblings.

As time passed, what little nurturing I received came more from them, through a bottle, than from my mother-and nothing at all from my father. I longed for the quiet days of closeness from my mother, the soft stroking of my hair and the beauty of her singing. But those moments were gone.

The energy in the household had moved down a dark road and any sense of peace was always interrupted by total chaos and negativity.

The slapping sound that had once marked my first breath of life now echoed through the home repeatedly as the darkness settled in upon the family. Smacking, yelling and violence became part of our daily life. I heard my mother's cries, my siblings' weeping, and felt the sadness that blanketed us all.

Hopelessness filled the air.

It seemed my mother had succumbed to the darkness and had given up. Perhaps it was some protective mechanism-a way to survive-but it didn't include me. Her distance left me aching. The days became long, dark, and empty. I was grateful for even the smallest kindness from my siblings, because I was helpless and needed them to survive. I would take anything remotely positive I could get.

One day as I slept in my crib, a glowing being appeared beside me and said, "Don't be afraid. I am Belleek, and I will protect you."

Even as a baby I could understand-not with words, but through thought. what was being relayed to me.

Suddenly I heard the vibrations from loud knocking and chaos at the front door. I recognized, from memories beyond this life, that I was in a house-a structure with doors and windows. Strangers burst in. I could hear a lot of yelling, screaming, and crying, it was just completely overwhelming.

Before I knew it, I was scooped into the arms of someone unfamiliar. My mother's screams and weeping echoed behind me, along with my siblings' cries. I felt the violent struggle between the stranger and one of my older siblings, who had always cared for me. But the stranger eventually won that unholy tug of war.

I was terrified. Then I was whisked away, torn from everything I knew and loved.

The sense of abandonment was immediate and complete.

My mother was gone. My siblings were gone. All that was familiar had been stripped away.

This was not how it was supposed to be.

Where was the love I craved, the compassion I needed, or the protection every newborn deserves? Instead, I was left behind-a victim of abuse, cruelty and neglect.

Even my siblings, despite their love and courage couldn't stop the chaos that swallowed us all. The violence, the screaming, the darkness-it never stopped. And finally, something beyond us stepped in. Strange outside forces removed us from the disaster we were drowning in.

As a baby, I couldn't understand the details, but I could feel the vibrational disruption, the loss and abandonment.

What should have been a beautiful beginning and an exciting wonderful new life, had turned into a storm of pain and fear.

None the less, down my new journeys road I would go for better or for worse.

OLD SOUL

I seemed to be moving in some sort of room while in an endless, uncomfortable nap in an upright position with straps holding me down. I was eventually awakened by the stranger and unhooked from my restraints, picked up, and taken from my moving capsule to a structure with a large statue of an angel in front of it. I recognized this image of an angel from long ago, and I knew I was in front of a building. There was a strangely familiar sound in the air, and off in the distance, I could hear faint sounds of older children nearby. Once inside, a figure of a woman who seemed to be like an angel but wearing an all-black robe with a slight silhouette of white surrounding her face came and retrieved me from the stranger who brought me there. That new, odd-looking angel comforted me, and I could feel the love and nurturing energy vibrating from her soul. She quickly began to feed and care for me, just as my older siblings had with a bottle. Even though I was hungry and thankful for the nourishment, I longed for the more loving touch of my mother's bosom. Exhausted from my uncomfortable trip, I finally relaxed and began to slowly drift off to sleep.

Later, when I awoke, I wondered about my new surroundings and whether I would ever feel true love from my mother again or fall peacefully asleep in her arms. As I gazed out the window next to my tiny crib, I saw as many sunrises and moons as possible as they came and went. I had no choice but to try and get used to my new surroundings. I was at least thankful for the love and compassion that I was being shown by my angel in black as time went by.

Sunrise after sunrise, I could feel myself growing and becoming stronger and more aware of my surroundings. I was always keenly aware of all the vibrations and frequencies that came to me throughout the day. I used them as a tool to help me perceive and understand the world around me. Some of the vibrational perceptions within me were ancient, and I always trusted them, even though I was not fully aware of why. Other vibrational perceptions in me were new and more of a learning experience. I continued forward, growing and becoming bigger and stronger, more intelligent and more perceptive with each sunset. I had a great sense of awareness of my surroundings and everything around me. I think it was something that stuck with me from the old times long ago in another life. I was always listening and feeling for the vibrational energy given off by everything around me, and I had a great understanding of language as well, even at a very young age.

One day, I could hear the arrival of someone new. I quietly peered around the corner of the room that I was in, and I could see a young man and a woman approaching the front desk. A soft, warm, familiar voice addressed those two new strangers and said, "Good afternoon, I'm Sister Bernadette, and welcome to Saint Gabriel's Orphanage." She said, "We are so pleased to have you here, and if there's anything at all that you need during your visit, please don't hesitate to ask. While you are visiting with the children, we want you to know that we consider our relationship a partnership between the children and their potential foster parents. The well-being of all our children here and moving forward is our top priority within this Catholic orphanage. Sister Marie will assist you on your tour and visits with the children today. God bless you and thank you for coming to visit us today." I watched and listened as our new strangers made their way about the orphanage, meeting and interacting with the other children there. I was a very intense observer, focused very much on the sounds and interactions on this unusual day. The new couple had eventually met a friend of mine, a little boy named Clarence, but he was extremely shy and scared of strangers, so the interaction was brief and did not seem to go so well. I was still quietly observing everything from the doorway of the library. It was a room that I often played in, and I found a great attraction to the pictures on the covers of the books as well as the various artwork on the walls around the room. I loved to draw as well, mostly birds and various other animals out in nature. There was always soft, calming music playing in the library too. I was particularly drawn to the peaceful sounds and the vibration that the music gave off. Eventually, Sister Marie led the couple into the library where I was cautiously observing the situation. Sister Marie was always so gentle and kind to me, and she said, "I have some nice people I would like you to meet." Then Sister Marie said to me, "This is Mary Storz and Ed Storz." I proceeded to reach my little hand out for a respectful greeting, as I was instructed to do in the past when we had visitors. The woman extended her hand to me, and I could feel immediately that she had a very kind and loving presence that illuminated from her face as she grasped my tiny hand. I could feel her energy, and it felt warm, positive, and full of love. The man stayed a bit more in the background and was not overly forward, which for me was a bit more comforting. Sister Marie said, "This is Sir William, but we like to refer to him as Will. He is two and a half years old." As the nice woman was about to speak to me, in a low little boy's voice, I quickly interrupted everyone and began pointing at the wooden molding on the door frame. I proceeded to explain to them that the wood was alive and pointed out the different animals that I could see in the grain of the wood. I also made mention of a nail that was protruding out because it was not fully hammered into the wood. The man suddenly stepped forward and was quite intrigued with my proclamation. He said to me, "I too see the life and the animals in the wood. Do you see the frog?" I excitedly said, "Yes, it's right there," as I pointed out the silhouette of the little frog that was drawn by nature in the grain of the wood. He said, "I love wood and nature, too. Perhaps I could teach you about all those things." He smiled and reached out his hand to me, and I did not hesitate to shake his hand. He had very large hands and huge arms with beautiful pictures on them. This was the first time that I had felt no fear from a man, and I felt comfortable sharing our ideas. Along with his kindness, I could sense a great positive strength vibrating from him. He had not only tremendous physical strength but a strong, positive inner strength as well. I felt extremely drawn to him, along with the woman too. Sister Marie laughed a little and said, "Well, I see we have two people with a very similar artistic vision." She then said to the couple, "As for Will, he beats to a different drum. In fact, he's what the old nuns here at the orphanage call an old soul. It's been many years since we've seen one like him. He's quite a rare commodity, perhaps a diamond in the rough." The woman knelt beside me and held my hand again and with a glowing smile said, "Will, you have the most beautiful blonde hair and blue eyes that I have ever seen—and those lashes, oh my Lord, those lashes. Would you like to come home with us? We could be your new mommy and daddy." I smiled and nodded with an affirming yes to her. I did not have to think twice about it, because it had been so long since I felt any sense of true love and protection that I was desperate for it, and this just felt right within my soul. There were smiles all around, and as we parted ways, everything about the visit felt right in my soul. I could hear Sister Marie tell them that it was the policy of the orphanage for the nuns not to allow themselves to get too close to any one child for fear of a bond that would eventually have to be broken again. They viewed themselves as the Lord's temporary caretakers of the most precious gifts. Sister Marie said she was very happy and hopeful for all of us. She also said that in the past, others had passed me by because they did not understand my intensity.

Excitedly, the young couple approached the front lobby, where Sister Bernadette, the Mother Superior, was awaiting them again. She said, "I see all smiles and feel that there is good news in the air—hopefully a blessing from the Lord above." Sister Bernadette then asked them if they had any other children, and they told her that they had one daughter about fifteen years older than Will. She replied, "That's absolutely wonderful." The young woman Mary then asked Sister Bernadette, "Is Will an only child?" Sister Bernadette replied, "No, he is one of six, and he is the youngest. All of Will's siblings are separated by two years, two brothers and three sisters. Unfortunately, all the children, because of age variations, could not be kept together, so they were split up within the system. From what I understand, the oldest sister Lona is with a family member, and his two older brothers, Jack and Jimmy, are together in a home for boys called Saint Francis. There are two remaining sisters, Maggie and Julie, who are together with another foster family." Mary then asked Sister Bernadette, "Can you tell us the circumstances that caused them to be put into the Catholic Social Services system?" Sister Bernadette then said, "I have a file here, and I'm not permitted to go into detail, but even for us, it's a bit of a gray area and difficult to completely understand the true nature of the circumstances that caused the breakup of the Campbell family. There had been various speculations of abuse, which were ongoing not only physically but mentally and sexually as well. There was further speculation of addiction issues, and then we got into some of the stranger areas of the Devil's work. There were hints of Satanism or satanic cult involvement and possibly even murder. Nonetheless, little Will came here because he was the youngest and the one with the least direct association to all that chaos. Because Will was removed at such a young age of six months, the authorities felt that he had suffered the least amount of damage." Mary was quite struck by all the information, but nonetheless, she felt confident in moving forward. Sister Bernadette informed Mary and Ed that the policy with Saint Gabriel's, under the guidance of Catholic Social Services, was for there to be a thorough home evaluation and a proper background check. If all went well, little Will would have a new home and a loving family. She said that it was also part of our policy for there to be monthly visits organized by Catholic Social Services for all foster parents, foster children, and possibly their other siblings and a biological parent or parents if permitted. Finally, all formal documents were then signed, and with a parting handshake from Sister Bernadette and the excited loving couple, the contract was started. As Mary and Ed quietly disappeared through the front door, I was left with anxious, hopeful feelings for what was coming for me.

Somehow, some way, out of nowhere, there seemed to be a glimmer of hope for me. I did not know what had become of my siblings, and I missed them and hoped that they too would be given a second chance in their lives. All I could do was wait and wonder about the possibilities that lay ahead for me. Was I going to be lucky—or yet again suffer tremendous disappointment, abandonment, and abuse as I continued forward on my new journey?

2

NEW HOME

Many days had passed since I met the young couple, and then finally one day, Sister Marie came in and told me that it was time to pack to go on an exciting new journey. I only had a very small suitcase and no toys to call my own. At the orphanage, the toys belonged to all the children, so I had to leave them behind. Before I knew it, I was greeted by another woman outside the orphanage who put me in the backseat of a car. This was my first time in a car since I was taken from my real family when I was a baby. I could still remember some of the feelings and the vibrations of the vehicle from when I was very young. I was a little timid about my journey but also very excited about what was coming for me.

It seemed as if a lot of time had passed during the drive, but eventually, we pulled up in front of a white house with green-trimmed windows and painted red bricks for the windowsills. There was a single big tree in the front yard with beautiful red leaves, and I admired it as we approached the front door. The woman proceeded to use the big metal knocker to knock on the front door, and then the door slowly opened. I could see the young couple, Mary and Ed, standing there with big smiles, and an energy of great excitement was all around me. The woman with me greeted them and said, "Hello. My name is Esther, and I will be Will's case worker; I'm looking forward to a great relationship with both of you." I too became very excited inwardly, but I did not show it outwardly. I still had a very natural cautious nature about me.

I remembered Mary as she knelt and gave me a warm, gentle hug while Ed was standing behind her. I couldn't believe it was going to be my new home, and I had no idea what to expect, but everything so far, felt good for me. Behind my new foster parents was another beautiful young girl. She was much older than me, but I could tell that she was not yet an adult. She too was very excited to see me and came forward and gave me a hug and said, "Hello, Will. My name is Liz, but you can call me Sissy." She said, "I'm going to be your new sister, and we are going to have fun."

While the adults were speaking, Liz said to me, "Would you like to see your new home?" I looked up at her and quietly nodded yes. She then gently took my hand and began to show me the room that we were in first, which was what she called the parlor, and it was quite large. The house was deceiving from the outside and did not look that large from the front until you entered it. There was a TV in the parlor, and the other thing I immediately noticed at the back of the room was a large fish tank, and I had never seen one before. I was immediately drawn to the water and the fish inside the tank. I thought it was the coolest thing I had ever seen. The fish tank was like a piece of nature inside your house. Liz said that the little fish in there were called guppies, and there were also a lot of little snails too.

There was also a big fish on the wall that Liz called Dad's bass, and two pictures of a mother dog and her puppies on each side of Dad's bass on the wall. Liz proceeded to grab my little suitcase and then said, "Let me show you to your new room." We walked down a very small hall off from the parlor to what would be my room on the left. The bedroom seemed so big to me, and I couldn't believe that I had all that space for myself, because at the orphanage, I shared a room with seven other little boys. There was a black and red rug on the floor and wood on the walls with a very distinct grain in the paneling. Immediately, I started to notice dinosaurs in the grain of the paneling on the walls. I said to Liz, "Look, there's a pterodactyl," and she laughed.

Then Liz quickly showed me the bathroom and my new foster parents' room, which was across the hall. She then led me by the hand, out to the kitchen, which was through a dining room. Then behind the kitchen was another room that Liz said was like her office. There was another big room at the back of the house that she called the outer kitchen. It was a beautiful room that sat up high, and there were huge windows across the back of it. You could look right out the windows up into the trees in the backyard. I thought it was just the coolest room with the best view.

She then showed me her room, which was upstairs. There was only one room upstairs, and it was her bedroom. I quickly spotted a bright pink phone on the floor, and I couldn't believe she had her own phone. I had never touched one, but I remembered that Sister Bernadette used to talk on the phone all the time.

Liz then said to me, "Come on, let me show you out back." As we went down another set of stairs, she said, "This is Dad's workshop." I was so amazed at all the tools everywhere. She told me to be sure not to touch anything unless Dad says it's OK, and I shook my head and nodded yes.

Next, we went out the back door, and I thought I had landed in paradise. It was so green everywhere, and there were so many trees. I only saw one tree at the orphanage on the playground there. I loved trees and was very drawn to them; I felt that I had a real connection to them.

There was a large fenced-in pen with a beautiful brown and white dog with long hair inside of the pen. Liz said, "This is Goldie, our Collie. She's out here during the day a lot, but she comes in at night." I had never seen a dog up close before, but I wasn't afraid of Goldie. She seemed nice, and Liz said, "She's a good old dog. You two will get along fine."

Behind the dog pen, I saw a small bridge that crossed a beautiful flowing little stream. I was amazed at all the life that was there. All I wanted to do was be near the water. There was so much life inside the creek—little fish, little water skeeters, and you could see frogs too! I was completely fascinated, and I thought that it was the most amazing place I had ever seen.

On the other side of the creek, there were so many trees everywhere. It was all woods, and Liz said, "That's all ours." All I wanted to do was go explore and touch the trees. Liz finally said, "We better go back in the house. We'll have plenty of time to explore later."

Liz smiled at me and said, "Let's go back inside and see everyone," then she took my hand and led me back into the house upstairs. When we got back into the parlor, the lady who drove me there in the car was gone, and Mary and Ed were standing there with wrapped presents in front of them. Mary said, "Will, these are for you." I wasn't sure what to do because I had never been given a present before.

Then Liz said, "It's OK, I'll help you open them. It'll be a fun surprise." Inside the gift boxes were lots of toys, such as little toy soldiers, toy animals, dinosaurs, and another box had a black-and-white big trash truck and a little bulldozer inside. There were other boxes too that had clothes inside for me to wear. There were so many clothes—I had never seen so many clothes before.

In my little suitcase that I brought, I only had two pairs of shorts along with two T-shirts, one set of dress pants and a dress shirt, plus my shoes. I was a bit overwhelmed, and I could hear Mary say to Ed, "I hope everything's OK. I know it will be an adjustment for Will." Everything for me was OK. I was very happy, but I was a deep thinker and an observer by nature. I was just taking it all in and trying to feel the vibrations in the energy of my new home, the yard, and everything else. I didn't always outwardly smile, and I often kept a serious face.

Mary knelt and looked at me and said, "Will, we want you to know that this is your home and you will always be loved and taken care of. We will always be here for you no matter what happens." No one had ever said that to me before. It felt good, and I did feel like I was at home. I leaned in and gave her a hug, and she looked at me again and said, if it's OK with you, you can call us Mom and Dad. What do you think about that?

I really didn't have to hesitate whatsoever. I smiled and nodded yes to Mary. Liz also said to please just call her Sissy, and I hugged her and said yes as well. I was happy to have a mom and dad; I really didn't know that kind of feeling of love until then. Mary smiled and gave me a hug and a kiss, and with that, my life had changed forever.

As time went by and I settled in, everything became a great sense of normalcy and a true family dynamic. I really loved exploring our house and playing with my new toys. I was only allowed in the backyard with supervision because I was still very young, and it was not good for me to wander off by the creek and the woods by myself yet.

I always longed to be near the water and the woods the most. Those areas had special energy around them—all the vibrations of nature along with the sounds and everything there just felt right for me. It was as if I had always been there, where I was meant to be. Something just pulled my soul there like a connection from a long distant time ago. Everything about my home, for the most part, had a good strong positive energy and a great vibrational feel to it.

The only exception would be, for some reason, I was afraid of the outer kitchen hall, which led to the steps headed down to the basement where my dad's workshop was. Maybe it was just the child in me, because it was a dark hall most of the time, and it seemed like a creepy area. However, something about that area of the house gave me quite a bit of fear.

At night when I went to sleep, I would take the bed sheet and wrap it around my head across the top of my head and ears and hold it very tight. For some reason, I felt safer that way, almost protected at night from anything bad or negative that I might be vulnerable to. That fear stayed with me for a very long time. I knew at a young age that I was blessed to be given a second chance, and I thrived on the opportunities that I had even as a young child every day.

My favorite thing when I was young was waking up on a beautiful day on the weekend, and then after breakfast, my dad would take me down to the little creek in the backyard. There we would walk along the creek, where I would chase frogs, little fish, and snakes. Eventually, I would learn to catch them and later release them back into their homes. For me, just being out in nature was where I felt I truly belonged, particularly near the water.

One day when we came back in the house, my mom said, "Well, how did it go boys?" My dad looked at her and said, "Will walks like an Indian. I've never seen a child do that before. It's as if he's been there a thousand years because he walks so quietly. Somehow, he just instinctively knows how to navigate along the creek very quietly and through the woods too. Will just for some reason has a great natural sense of nature and that whole environment. There's a real intensity about him that's different than other children."

My mom said, "Well, he is a special boy, and we are lucky to have him in our lives."

The years would slowly roll by in my happy little life, and I was growing stronger and becoming smarter and more aware of everything around me. I had a great sense of intuitiveness and a strong connection to all the vibrational energy all around me. I also was blessed with a wonderful group of friends in the neighborhood.

My group of friends was not real big there, but we did everything together—from playing sports to various games and exploring out in nature. I taught my friends how to catch all the little creatures in the creek behind my house, and we shared many fun days together. I never spoke to any of my friends about how I was so greatly affected by all the vibrational energy around me. When I was with them, I was just a friend and another ordinary kid in the neighborhood.

Down the street from our house, there was a much larger creek called Neshaminy Creek. It was a tributary that fed into the Delaware River further down below. It was tidal water, so there was high tide and low tide there.

When I was about six years old, my dad decided to take me fishing one day at Neshaminy Creek. It was a life-changing event for me. I was in awe of it when I looked around at all the water, the wildlife, and the giant ancient rocks. For some reason, I felt that I belonged there and that I had been there long ago. I somehow knew that place and connected very deeply with it.

My very first fish that I caught was an eel. I was so excited that I pulled it in so hard, it slapped me in the face—and that was my baptism to fishing. From that day forward, fishing would forever become my favorite thing to do. Everything about it felt right. All the vibrational energy was perfect for me—from the rippling of the flowing water to the sound of the breeze through the trees and all the wildlife. I greatly enjoyed the occasional crashing of a fish leaping out of the water too. It was a place of total peace for me.

My dad used to point out that the giant boulders and many other things about that place had been the same since the days of the Indians. Somewhere very deep in my soul, I already knew that the Indians had lived along that waterway. I could feel their energy run through me as I did my quiet Indian walk along that Neshaminy Creek. While I was observing all the wildlife there, I always had a complete sense of contentment, as all that new and ancient vibrational energy surrounded me. It too felt like a long-lost home for me.

I was truly grateful for the opportunity of a happy, loving, prosperous life given to me by my foster family—Ed, Mary, and Sissy. I was at total peace in my soul, and I did not take any of it for granted. I knew I was the lucky one, and I was very aware that most foster kids did not have the amazing opportunity that I was blessed with.

Late at night before I fell asleep, I would often wonder about the outcome of my siblings, especially Maggie and Julie. I hoped that they were all OK too, but I also felt a deep, nagging uneasiness about their situations on their journeys.

NEW SIGHT

When I was about eight years old, I struggled as usual to get myself up one morning. I was always quite a bit later waking up than all my friends. I headed straight to the kitchen to whip up some oatmeal and hot Red Rose tea. I always drank my tea straight up, because I was always too tired to bother to put cream and sugar in it. I really loved to sit in the outer kitchen, which overlooked our beautiful backyard. The large windows in the outer kitchen had a direct view right into the canopy of a large chokecherry tree. There was a little pink birdhouse, which sat directly in line with my view of the canopy. It was always nice to see what little birds had made their new home in there that year. I also had a great view of the dog pen, where Goldie resided during the day. It was such an incredibly beautiful, warm summer morning—the kind of morning that would entice any eight-year-old to head straight to the backyard, out into nature, and venture along the creek. There was always so much anticipation of seeing all the amazing creatures that lived there along the creek.

I finished breakfast and headed down to the back porch to sit and observe the beautiful things that nature had to offer me. That day would be my first recollection of any major type of visual intuitiveness—or, as some would say, to foresee something. As usual, I was sitting on the back porch gazing out into the backyard down in front of me. There were many large trees around the yard and high above the dog pen as well. Probably a good fifty feet or so, the branches of the trees would intertwine from one tree to the next. Squirrels had trails within the trees that they followed; they generally didn't just randomly run through the trees. The squirrels would always use those pathways every day. Of course, the squirrels were very sure-footed animals, and they were very comfortable in that environment, up within the trees. I had never seen a squirrel ever fall from a tree, but this day would be different. I could feel the energy shift around me as a small glowing orb appeared before me. As it came closer to me, I could see what looked like a glowing face within the orb. I was not afraid but felt a sense of comfort and familiarity from this orb. I suddenly received communication from the orb, but there was no actual speaking—it was just a sense of knowing through thought that said, "Remember to see." I then had a quick vision come to me of a squirrel making his way through the trees and across the main branch high above the dog pen. Goldie hated the squirrels and always wanted to get them because she was being taunted by the squirrels every day. In this vision, suddenly out of nowhere, the squirrel slipped off the branch and fell into the dog pen. Somehow, the squirrel not only landed on its feet but also narrowly escaped Goldie's jaws, ready and waiting to devour him! Less than a minute after the vision I had—sure enough—there came that squirrel through the trees, up and over the branch above the dog pen. Then, just like the vision, the squirrel slipped off the branch and fell exactly as I previously saw it! The little squirrel also fell on his feet and narrowly escaped my dog, Goldie. It was identical to my premonition! It was as if I was being tested or reminded of something important by the strange orb. I was never able to forget that little event, and it would be just the tip of the iceberg for me moving forward. Over time, many other unusual, similar things would come and unfold before me.

The only person that I had ever confided in regarding those sorts of things when I was young was my wonderful Aunt Jean. She was the wife of my dad's brother Rob, and really one of the most beautiful souls that I had ever met in my life. Aunt Jean had the biggest, most beautiful eyes that looked right through you when she was speaking to you. People often said that eyes were the windows to the soul, and I very much believed that to be true as well. You could most definitely read a lot in a person's eyes. My Aunt Jean had many visions throughout her life of things that would happen around her—and particularly with family members too. I don't think many people believed a lot of what she would say, but I always knew it to be true. She certainly was in touch with a very deep vibrational undercurrent all around her. Visions came to her in pieces, kind of like a puzzle. Sometimes she would draw things and even call and warn family members that she thought would be in harm's way. Because of her gifts and great loving personality, I was able to connect with her and speak to her as a child about the various things that I could see and feel as well. I never told anyone about that, and it stayed between me and her our whole lives. She always told me not to be afraid of it—that it was a gift from the glowing angels. My Aunt Jean was the matriarch of her side of the family for sure. She had a great sense of compassion, love, and understanding of all people. She truly understood life and the tremendous importance of being a family. She was my favorite relative for sure, and her son Greg was most definitely my number one cousin. Greg was really a brother to me and always would be.

I was learning to understand some of the deep impressions that I was feeling and connecting with from possibly very long ago. I was blessed to have my Aunt Jean in my life as someone who could guide me to help navigate and comprehend the vibrational energy that we both were sensitive to. To me, she was a special gift to help me interpret the spiritual, intuitive gifts that followed me through my young life as I embraced all that was around me.

LITTLE WATER SIGN

I was born on November 5, 1963. Yep, I was a little Scorpio and very much true to form; however, many people didn't realize that Scorpios—and other signs—came into the world at different levels. I was what the old nuns would call an old soul, and I had been here a few times in the journey we called life. I still carried the same characteristics and traits as all Scorpios, but in a much deeper form. It was in my Scorpio nature to sit back and observe all my surroundings. All my decisions were made by deeply evaluating a situation or following my intense intuitive instincts forged long ago. As my dad would always say about me, even as a very small child, "Will was very intense." Intuition was just one of the characteristics of a Scorpio—and especially an old one like me.

From a very young age and as far back as I remembered, I always had a great attraction to any water. Being near it, hearing it, feeling it, and admiring all the life it gave was intoxicating for me. It always gave me a great sense of calmness, contentment, and wonderment. To me, the vibrational energy around water was harmoniously perfect. It was no surprise for a Scorpio, being that I was a true water sign. I literally spent countless hours along that little creek in my backyard, which was a small tributary called the Queen Anne Creek. The little creek flowed down the street into the larger Neshaminy Creek, and the Neshaminy Creek flowed into the Delaware River, then off into the great Atlantic Ocean.

Throughout my entire childhood, I would always love to watch and observe every form of wildlife around the creeks, and of course, I became a very active fisherman. I never ever got bored of fishing; I could sit there all day even if I wasn't catching anything. The simple peace from the experience was truly worth it for me. When I wasn't fishing, I would often just wander along Neshaminy Creek or even walk in the water to feel more in harmony with all the life within it. I was also very attracted to the huge ancient boulders around and in the creek. I would often sit on them to feel their old vibrational energy. I would imagine myself on the boulders long ago, at a different time, and I could feel how much was still the same and timeless.

A few times a year, my dad and grandfather would take me fishing off the New Jersey coast in the Atlantic Ocean. Being in a boat in that massive ocean and fishing was the ultimate connection to water for me. The ocean grounded me, despite its ability to humble any person with its seemingly endless and vast energy. It was a place where life and death were so close, yet beautifully in perfect harmony and balance. I would get so excited to go on the fishing trips to the ocean that I could barely sleep the night before. I also had the opportunity to catch bigger, stronger fish out in that beautiful ocean. Whenever I needed to unwind or in times of great stress from traumatic events in my life, I would always go to the water to reclaim that peace again.

Water was undoubtedly the lifeblood of our beautiful, glorious Mother Earth. Nothing could exist without it. All life as we understood it was in perfect harmony with it. Whether it was in its violent form or peaceful form, it was always a necessary constant. Water always grounded me and kept me connected to the Earth, with just the slightest vibrations in its current. Ah yes, me and the water were always in total peace and harmony.

Those were the times when I honed that new yet seemingly old intuitive sight within myself. As I slowly became more open vibrationally and spiritually, I forged my connection to the Earth and allowed myself to feel all that surrounded me on a much deeper level. A new beginning of awakening and universal awareness was starting to open for me. As I continued to get older, I had no idea how much more intense everything would become for me. I looked ahead with great anticipation of what was to come as my life would continue to unfold. I was not fully aware of just how perfect a natural candidate I was for all the mysterious vibrational interactions to come in everything I would experience on my own unique journey.

3

THE VISITS

Once a month, I had to go for mandatory family visits organized by Catholic Social Services at a big round Sheraton hotel in Center City Philadelphia. For me, I could always feel a shift in the energy around me, because I was uncomfortable going on the visits. I absolutely hated disrupting my peaceful, everyday life to go into a city atmosphere that I despised. Unfortunately, I had no choice in the matter and was forced to comply with the rules of the Catholic Social Services foster system.

While on the visits, two of my biological sisters, Maggie and Julie, were always there, and occasionally my real mother would show up as well. My oldest sister or my brothers were not there. I never felt comfortable with the visits, and I hated going. It really had nothing to do with seeing my real sisters—I enjoyed seeing them. It had more to do with the uneasiness and discomfort I felt around my real mother. It was hard to describe, but I felt like we were opposites, coming from different ends of the spectrum, so to speak. She had a dark, negative energy to me, and any sense of a loving mother that I felt as a baby was long gone. She didn't pay much attention to me and usually spent the time speaking to my foster dad, Ed. My foster mom, Mary, never went on those mandatory visits. I think it was just too difficult for her because we were a closely bonded family. She always feared that I would be taken away from her. The vibrational energy I felt there was uncomfortable and confusing. I spent most of the time playing with Julie since she was only two years older than me. The visits were torture for me every month. To even have to put myself through that was painful. After all, I was content at home with the family who cared for and loved me. I didn't want any interruptions in what I felt was my normal life.

When I was about nine years old, my oldest brother, Jack, came on a visit. The vibrational energy coming off him was a lot like mine. He too, I could feel, was very creative and a deep thinker. Jack and I sat together on a park bench outside the hotel and talked—it was nice, and he felt positive to me. He proceeded to quickly sketch a statue in the park of a man on a horse. I was amazed by how good and quick he was at drawing art. He gave the rolled-up sketch to me as a keepsake. I really liked him, but unfortunately, I would never see him again. I never had the opportunity to meet my other brother, Jimmy. Sometimes, when it was time to leave the visits, my dad Ed would drive my real mom home, so she didn't have to take a bus. I can remember driving along a big river with stone-arch bridges everywhere, and she lived in a little brick house not far from the river. I could only focus on getting back home, where things felt normal and I could be happy again.

There was one visit where the vibrational energy I was feeling was particularly negative and uncomfortable. Somehow, my real mother snuck me away from the hotel and took me back to her house. I was really scared and uncomfortable there with her. I think my real father may have been there as well because I could feel that overwhelming negative presence I remembered from when I was very young. There was a familiar tenseness in the air with screaming and yelling—just like when I was a baby. I eventually kept putting my hands over my ears to block out the negative sounds of chaos. Then, as I was drifting off to sleep, I could feel the vibrational energy around me shift as a glowing being presented itself to me. The glowing being told me that his name was Dagda, my protective guardian, and assured me that I would be okay and protected once again. There were no actual words spoken, but I completely understood the information he was giving me through thought. Somehow, I knew Dagda from long ago, so I completely trusted what he was relaying to me. After what was probably about a week, the authorities came and removed me yet again from the house to return me back to my foster parents. I was a bit traumatized by the whole situation and wouldn't speak for quite a while. I always sat to the left of my dad Ed at the dinner table, and after that event, I reached over and put my right hand on his left forearm on top of his eagle tattoo. I always felt safe and protected when I was with him. Once I started doing that, our bond grew even stronger, and I could tell that he understood how important his level of protection and guidance was for me. So, from that moment on, we would be totally connected for eternity. All the energy coming from my dad Ed, as well as my mom Mary and sister Liz, was always positive and full of complete love. It was all I ever really needed.

My mom Mary gave herself to me completely. She was very engaging with me, especially when I was very young. Mary would always celebrate all the seasons and all the yearly holidays and make it so exciting. Mary had different decorations that went on the windows to celebrate either a particular holiday or a season of the year. I always looked forward to helping her decorate. Mary also taught me how to make cookies and cook simple dishes. She would tell me how important those life skills were for me as I grew older. My mom also taught me how to sew, and it was a great lifelong skill to have. She was a perfect mom to me, and I loved her very much.

Sissy was the perfect sister for me too. Even though she was a lot older than me, she always spent time with me, and in many ways, she was like another mom in the house. If I wanted something that my mom and dad were hesitant about, Sissy always found a way to get it for me. We never even had a single fight over anything. She was a tremendous blessing to me as well.

When I was in sixth grade, about ten years old, after what seemed like an endless amount of time being exhausted by those visits, I declared to the teacher in my Catholic grade school that my last name would now be Storz, not Campbell. Because of legal guidelines, I had been using my real last name, Campbell, in school and then using my foster last name, Storz, once I got home. Apparently, there must have been some sort of meeting between Mary and Ed and the principal and teachers about my proclamation. From the next day forward, my name in school would be Will Storz. That sort of unconventional thing could never have happened in a public school. However, in the 1970s within the Catholic School System, they allowed it, even with no legal binding.

In fact, my real mother would never relinquish the rights for my legal adoption to Mary and Ed. I continued to use my foster parents' last name of Storz all the way into high school. My friends at home who were in my high school probably thought it was odd, but they never said anything to me about the two different last names. The truth was that Will Storz never really existed legally, but nonetheless it happened. While I was in high school, when I was sixteen years old, I stopped going on the mandatory visits. I assumed that I could do it legally without any repercussions, and it somehow worked out in my favor. That was the absolute end to the visits for me, and at that time, it was the right decision for me.

I finally had complete separation from my real family, and I could just be Will Storz. I was happy and content with my decision. It never had anything to do with my two sisters, Maggie and Julie; it was just a sense of peace that I needed in my soul. The vibrational energy around me felt much more in balance, as I would, for the time being, be leaving the Campbell name behind me.

4

DAD'S WORKSHOP

My dad's workshop was in my mind a very solemn place. It was a place of great creativity, peace and learning for me. It was also hallowed ground for me and my dad, and a place of great communication and trust between us. The workshop with my dad was where much of my early creativity would begin to emerge. So many of his teachings would come from the shop. It molded me and began a lasting imprint on my soul.

My dad Ed grew up in a very hard life but always had a great underlying talent for working with wood and cabinetmaking. He was attracted to wood crafting from a very young age. The very first thing that he ever built was a tiny round wooden footstool, with his name and the date engraved on the underside. He worked extremely hard at various factory jobs that were very long hours and had little pay. Eventually he finally caught a break and got a job loading trucks down along the river front in Philadelphia. He said it nearly killed him the first week because the work was so difficult on his body. Then to his utter amazement when he received his first paycheck, my dad and my mom danced around the house because they couldn't believe how much money it was. They thought they were going to be rich. It was funny how just a little could seem like a lot more to some people, depending on their situations in life. He would then learn through other guys on the job how to drive a truck and eventually made that his lifelong career. Although the pay was a very good union wage with great stability for a hard-working man; his underlying talents always nagged him, and he longed to release the great creativity that was inside of him. He did many woodworking projects on the side, mostly for family members and a few other people. He built some beautiful and wonderful cabinets and hutches and various other forms of great woodworking. Unfortunately, his soul was restless, because he really wanted to work with wood as his career. He had a chance when he was young to work with his uncle Bob, who was a great lifelong master carpenter. Uncle Bob had noted that the first time he saw Ed's work, how incredible it was for a man who had not grown up in the trade. He offered to guide my dad into the business and help him along. However, life unfortunately got in the way of his dreams and my dad just could not risk the stability for his family. So, he sacrificed his dreams to provide for his family and give them the stability they needed throughout his life. He regretted that decision for his own soul for his whole life but in another way, he was not sorry that he had provided for his family.

I was always alongside my dad in the shop, from about three years old on through a lot of my early life. He mostly played old country and western music, and we would even act out a Marty Robins song called, Mr. Shorty. Singing, creating and life knowledge was always the general theme in the woodshop. I was always learning basic skills of hammering and screwing things together and many other various types of wood working techniques that he taught me. My dad would always say to me "Will my boy, I'll teach you all the skills that I know; it's important for a man to know how to do things in this world and to do them properly with pride." I gobbled up every scrap of what I could, and I always had a little side project that I would build alongside him. He always provided the knowledge and helped me whenever I needed it. He taught me all the skills of woodworking but because of my wandering mind; it appeared to him as though I was not paying attention or really grasping everything he was telling me. Even though I was building all these things right under his nose, he missed my attention to detail and tremendous focus. My dad had a special little electric tool tucked away on the second shelf of his work bench for me. It was wrapped up in newspaper, and he promised to give it to me when I got older and was responsible enough to handle a tool with power. I never did get the tool from him; I guess he didn't think that I had paid attention enough, because my mind was always wandering on many different things that were creative.

I always made my family Christmas presents out of the scraps of wood that my dad had left over from various jobs he was working on. One of the most important things I learned from my dad when it came to woodworking was his natural sense and understanding of the spirit of the wood. He taught me to always look at the wood very closely. He told me that all wood had a story of its life and its struggles if you looked at how it grew. The right piece of wood had to be selected for the right part of whatever it was that you were creating. He believed that we had a deep underlying connection with the wood through nature. I learned about different types of woods and trees and how they grew. He always said to be patient when selecting your wood, the right piece and connection to what you were creating would present itself to you in the proper time. Even though he taught me so much, I still had this sort of knowing deep inside me of the wood and its place in nature when it was still a tree. It was a very old sense of knowledge that was deep within me from long ago.

My dad had a deep spiritual side that he always shared with me as well. It was most unusual for a person coming from the inner city and not really growing up around a lot of nature. He always told me about how connected he was with wolves as well. He even referred to himself as the wolf. He said that as a kid he would sneak off to the parks in the city of Philadelphia to fish and enjoy the peacefulness of nature. I believe that was where he learned to be one with nature and became in touch with his higher spiritual self. One of my dad's great sayings was, "Take your time and never rush a job; better to be done correctly the first time and always take pride in what you do, no matter how small the task." He would also say, "Wood carries life within it, even after the tree is cut down and repurposed." He told me that a forest of trees has a whole element of communication between them that is unseen by most people. Even though his teachings were all priceless to me, I still already understood much of this from a deep underlying current within me. Some of those ancient ways of looking at the spirit of trees were just starting to be talked about slightly in the mainstream, for those who would bother to listen. It was theorized that long after a tree is cut down and just a stump, it continued to be nourished and supported for quite some time under the ground by the surrounding trees. They were all connected and shared a common vibrational life force amongst them and the Earth. What a beautiful thing that it was to think about—oh, if only humans could have been so unconditionally supportive of each other and the Earth.

I'd say even as a child, I could tackle most mechanical tasks put before me or that I had thought of in my mind. My dad Ed would even bring home bikes and skateboards and other things from his friends at work, for me to repair for their kids. I was pretty much handy all around, including electronics and electrical work. However, my dad was not comfortable with electric work. I was always a very big dreamer as a kid; I even tried to turn a go-kart that we had built together into an actual driving car! When I was about eight years old, I even built an airplane that from a distance anyone could tell what it was, as rough as it may have been. I also took a chinstrap off an old football helmet, then I put the helmet on and climbed inside the airplane and pretended to fly it. I always had a very big imagination. My dad took a picture of me in that little wooden airplane at the time I was pretending to fly it. Years later, he pulled out a few hundred pictures that had been stored around the house and casually said to me, "Do you know what my favorite picture is?" It could've been any one of many pictures taken over the years. But quickly my natural Scorpio intuitive instincts kicked in, and I said of course I do—it's the one of me sitting in the little airplane that I built. It had to be that one, because it displayed an element of innocence, creativity, a sense of being free and craftsmanship. I kind of chuckled to myself, because I knew there was no way he was going to stump me on which picture it was out of all of them. I could just feel what was the correct answer with everything deep inside of me. I had no idea as a kid how much all those woodworking and technical skills and creative thoughts would carry with me my entire life. Eventually it would mold me into who I would become much later in my adult life. My eyes and instincts would always see things in a different form than what seemed normal to most people. I was very good at repurposing various things. I could always see something for a new gadget that had nothing to do with the original purpose of the object at all. If I was walking through any store, I would always look at things differently. Even if it was just a plastic bowl, I would think, well, this could be used for something completely different and just be able to make it work. That was my instinctive creative nature and just how I was wired.

When I would play and pretend as a young child in the early 1970s, I always wanted to be the Indian and not the cowboy. I quietly navigated my imaginary Indian world as I would creep along the water or through the woods. It just felt right to me, and I somehow knew how to build all kinds of various Indian things. I would make my own authentic tomahawks and various realistic Indian knives. I also instinctively knew how to make my own bow and arrows. I knew just the right branch to grab for the bow that was strong but flexible enough to shoot. I also knew the perfect weed that grew strong and straight for making awesome arrows too. No one had ever taught me those Indian tool-making skills, but somehow, I did it with precision and great authenticity. Me pretending to be the little Indian just came natural to me, so I just embraced it, and I felt at peace when I played like that. My friends were always cowboys, and I was okay with that, because I was always a bit of a little rebel anyway.

All those things were just natural for me, and I loved being able to create the things that I visualized in my mind. I trusted my instincts and the deep vibrational foresight with anything I created. I suppose I was always not only creative but deeply in touch with all my surroundings to allow my creativity to happen. I just had a great sense of knowing how to do a lot of various things that I learned from my dad and some other things from some older self, deep within me. I had a true connection from the visualizations in my mind to my hands to build or fix many different things. It must have just been some deep vibrational intuitiveness that gave me some of the skills that I had and just naturally understood. I couldn't exactly explain how I absorbed and understood everything I did. All that knowledge would not only shape my childhood but would carry with me throughout my journey moving forward in life.

5

MUSIC

Music and the vibrational energy from it were always a big part of my life in some form or another. When I was a very young child, probably three to four years old, I would go out into my favorite room, the outer kitchen that overlooked our beautiful backyard. I would play with the string that hung down to open and close the curtains. The end of the string had a little plastic cup on it, and that was what I would use as my pretend microphone. I really didn't even know what a microphone was at that age. But I would sing into it, and I always had perfect pitch and a good voice. The tremendous attraction to music and anything that made sound was intoxicating for me. The wonderment of music and sound just intensified in me as I got older.

My first introduction to a real instrument was the piano in our family's room known as the parlor. My sister Liz was fifteen years older than me, and she could play the piano quite well. The piano was a little spinet, which is the smallest type of vertical upright piano. It was built by a company called Lester, a local piano maker in the Philadelphia region up through the late 1950s. It wasn't a great piano, but it played and sounded decent to me. I was completely attracted to the sound of that piano and its vibrational energy from the frequencies it produced.

For some reason, I could just play from a young age without a single lesson. Even at around six, I could pick out songs that were in my head, starting with just single-note versions. I had a whole group of Christmas carols that I would sit and play with too. The first song I ever played was What Child Is This, an old traditional Christmas carol.

Unfortunately, my mom and dad had no clue if I was really playing, because they were not musical in any way, and my sister Liz never really acknowledged my playing abilities at all. Maybe it was because I was able to play by ear, and she had to read music. I'm not sure why I could play the way I did; it just came naturally to me.

My grandpop, Pat McAlinden, on my foster mom's side, was the only musical one in the family. He played harmonica and what they would call the squeezebox, a small version of the accordion back in the day. My grandpop loved music and would play with his buddies when he was younger out in the bars—otherwise known as the taproom. When I was about eight years old, he taught me to play the harmonica, but my grandmom, Milly McAlinden, was always yelling at him to stop making so much noise. Unfortunately, she had no concept of musicianship and didn't quite appreciate it at all. I loved her very much—she was an awesome woman—but she would always nag him about playing music.

Later down the road, when I was about twelve years old, I gave my grandpop an excellent German harmonica that I bought for him as a Christmas gift. After he passed away many years later, I got it back to keep for myself. It was something that always reminded me of him, his teachings, and his love of music.

I have to say, the thing that I was most musically attracted to at a young age was most definitely the drums. One Christmas, I received a fantastic gift from my parents. They bought me a little red toy drum set with cheap cardboard drumheads. I loved them and beat the heck out of them, but I kept tearing up the drumheads because they were so cheaply made—that was all my parents could afford.

The deep creative thinker that I was quickly decided to make my own drum set out in our shed next to the house. As it turned out, it became quite a cool set of drums and had a very good sound. To build it, I used an old heavy plastic trash can turned upside down for my bass—or what drummers called a kick drum. I then used a variety of drywall buckets and cans around the house for my other drums, called toms, to create various sounds. I made the two drumsticks out of a fiberglass three-foot flagpole. I cut the flagpole in half, and it worked perfectly.

I would play those drums for hours, and since I was outside the house, I thought I wasn't driving my mom too crazy. However, eventually, my mom would yell at me to stop making all that loud noise.

I understood that, historically, other than the human voice, the drum was the oldest instrument on the planet. An ancient inner sense within me knew that drums dated back centuries, to the beginning of our known history. Drumming could unlock a basic vibrational level of movement within us and all the things that surrounded us. For this reason, many ancient cultures used it as a tool for deeper spiritual connection to the Earth and the Universe. The same kinds of rituals still occur in modern times.

The truth of the matter was, even as a young lad, I understood that everything around us on our planet had a deep underlying vibrational connection. I recognized that this connection tied all living and non-living things together, like a web of pathways between all the elements we lived with. I could also sense that the vibrations covered a large range, from very low to very high. Most vibrations were not perceived by most people. However, I connected to those vibrations. I could feel things, perceive things, and even foresee what others could not. What a truly blessed gift I was given to be able to see and comprehend life in that way.

All those feelings carried with me as I grew older into my early teens. That vibrational energy may have been hard for some people to grasp, and for the close-minded naysayers, maybe not even relevant at all. I strongly felt that people needed to pay attention to the subtle things all around them and to the glorious gifts that nature had to offer us. Those vibrational feelings were very real to me, and I understood that there was most definitely an underlying vibrational bond between everything.

I felt sorry for those who had no connection to that whatsoever, because I felt they were missing out on the real fundamentals of life. I believed that all the energy around us kept us grounded as spiritual and physical beings. As my dad would always say, "Pay attention to Mother Nature and listen to her and all of her magnificent things, because they are one with all of us." For many of us, it was what we referred to as God or a higher being connection.

As a young teen, I became even more aware that most humans were, unfortunately, disconnected from higher consciousness and any earthly spiritual connection. The old soul within me somehow kept feeding me knowledge that, as a society, we had slowly lost over the centuries. Our minds had expanded vastly from a logical and technical standpoint, but we had lost our connection to the Earth and those important vibrational energies. We sadly allowed them to drift off deep into our subconscious, because we were too focused on what we could see in the obvious world.

Most of humanity functioned like a horse with blinders on. They could only perceive what was right in front of them. I knew that animals had that important connection to the Earth and relied on it, allowing themselves to be one with it. Some ancient feelings within me could see it clearly, but most people failed to even recognize it. People who understood those concepts and truly lived by them were generally very peaceful souls and content with their lives. Unfortunately, most people lived in a scattered mental state, full of various forms of aggression and frustration, ruled by meaningless things in their lives.

I too was guilty of the scattered mind from time to time because of life's struggles. However, I could always rely on myself to be grounded and return to what we fundamentally were long ago. Music, in any form, I believe, helps us connect to higher consciousness and can be very grounding. Music is everywhere around us. I always wished people would just listen to the true magical sounds of the Earth. I had a deep vibrational connection inside me that I always felt came from ancient times, though I never fully understood why. The spiritual connections I felt from nature's music were calming, and it was always like a door opening to lead me back down the correct path of life.

LOVE OF THE GUITAR

At around sixteen years old, I started playing guitar seriously, but that wasn't my first time touching one. One Christmas, when I was nine years old, my mom and dad bought me a little cheap acoustic guitar. It was made of wood and functioned well. I was immediately drawn to it, and after we finished our normal morning Christmas routine at our house, we went to my grandparents' house to celebrate. I would often fall asleep there because there usually wasn't a lot to do. They always had the heat cranked way up, and it made me extremely tired. I knew that guitar would keep me busy for sure. Honestly, I loved playing it there, even though I had no idea how to really play it correctly. Amazingly, just like with the piano, I could pick out songs on it the very first time I picked it up. I figured out how to play some of the Christmas carols that I played on the piano on that guitar as well. Once again, no one noticed, I was just a kid sitting in the corner making a lot of noise. Nobody had a clue about my newfound skill, except maybe my Grandpop Pat, the only other active musician.

So, when I was sixteen, that's when guitar got serious for me. One day, my good friend Jay, who lived up the street from me, was playing a guitar in his driveway through an amplifier. He had been taking guitar lessons for quite some time. I thought it was cool, and I was instantly drawn to its vibrational energy. Another kid a few houses up from Jay, named Danny, for some reason had a couple of old electric guitars at his house. I think they belonged to an older relative. Danny got his hands on them and brought them down to Jay's to fool around with. Danny couldn't play a lick, but I was eyeballing those guitars for sure. I somehow managed to talk them into letting me take Danny's two electric guitars back to my house to fool around with, and man, was I excited when I pulled off the deal. One guitar was a real cheapie called a Harmony. It had a black body with a sunburst finish and a bad neck with super high string action, which made it harder to play. The other guitar was a cool kit guitar that somebody put together with a multitude of electronics in it. It had a much better neck and a way bigger variety of tones you could get out of it. For some reason, I started off playing the crappy electric one while sitting in an old beach chair on my parents' back porch. As always, I went straight to picking out a tune, and in fact, I remember the first song I ever played. It was on the radio at the time—a real sappy ballad called With You I'm Born Again. Oh brother, I couldn't believe that was my first song on electric guitar. I wasn't even plugged in because I didn't have an amp yet. I hadn't worked out that deal, but I was planning on getting Jay's amplifier as soon as I could.

Because I liked the guitar so much, I decided that guitar lessons might be a good thing for me. I thought about it for a while and decided that if I were to study classical guitar, that would be more difficult than traditional lessons and probably more beneficial. I figured if I could play classical guitar, I could play anything. So, I chose the harder route, believing it would give me better results. I talked to my sister Liz about it, and she did a little research and found a guy about twenty minutes from our home who gave classical guitar lessons. Liz paid for my lessons and signed me up—she was always an awesome sister! I had a slight problem though—I needed an acoustic guitar to take those lessons. You couldn't learn classical guitar with an electric. I had to think fast. Ah-ha! I remembered Sissy had an old acoustic guitar that had sat in her office for years. The guitar was mahogany brown, and I had never once seen her pick it up or even attempt to play it—but there it was, just waiting for me. So off I went to the office to snatch it up, quick as a lick. The strings were all rusty and messed up, and I noticed the bridge of the guitar was coming off. At first, I thought it was going to be a problem, but I didn't worry too much. I figured I could repair it. I quickly ran to Dad's workshop to make a new bridge. I cut a new one even though I really had no idea what I was doing, but Dad had taught me great woodworking skills, and I was confident I could make it work. Oh, and while I was at it, I decided to change the finish to make it look cool and modern. I painted the guitar black in a blue sunburst style. Afterwards, Sissy took me to the local music store to get new strings—folk-style guitar strings. They weren't classical strings, but not steel strings either; they were kind of a crossover style. After I put the new strings on, I was ready to learn classical guitar! Oh, and I also had no idea how to tune the guitar either.

Soon, I was off to my first lesson to meet the guitar teacher, Mr. Garrett. Sissy graciously offered to drive me there as well. Mr. Garret lived in an old ranch house at the back of a housing development. When the door opened—wow—a very bizarre-looking guy with coke-bottle glasses popped out like some psycho cartoon character. The glasses made his eyeballs look so big, he appeared to have landed on Earth from another planet. I swear he had big alien eyes, just staring at me out of those massively thick lenses. He smiled and said, "Welcome, Will." Mr. Garrett was a real quirky guy; he would always turn his head in odd positions while looking at you—kind of like a dog when you ask it a question. I thought, Man, this guy's got something wrong with him physically and mentally for sure. But if he could teach me to play guitar, then I was all in. I managed to get through the formal introductions, and now it was time for my first lesson. I was very excited. Then my guitar guru pulled out his instrument—wow! It was a ten-string classical guitar—six normal strings, plus four bass strings, with a neck about six inches wide. Mr. Garrett was a great guitar player and a former classical concert guitarist. Unfortunately, he told me he had damaged his tendons overstretching for notes beyond his physical limits. Because he didn't have big hands, the injury ended his concert career. So, Mr. Garrett was stuck living in that dumpy little house, with a couple of ankle biting kids running around and junk everywhere. Oh well, that was his problem—I didn't care, if that creepy twin-eyed cyclops could take me to guitar god status.

So, it was time to show him my guitar, and I was so proud of my brilliant repair work. One glance from old bug-eyes, and I could see deep concern on his face. "First things first," he said with an anguished look. "We must tune this guitar." As he began tuning my masterpiece, I saw it was going to be a serious challenge. I hadn't factored in the tension that a guitar bridge is under. You could hear it cracking and lifting as he turned the pegs. The whole scene was scary. I thought, oh man, just get me through this lesson. I felt like I could fix the guitar better next time in Dad's shop. Mr. Garrett managed to get it somewhat in tune, even though the bridge had lifted in the back, it hadn't fully ripped off yet. I could see it was going to be a shaky lesson, and the fear of the bridge flying off and cracking one of us in the skull was real!

The lesson began, and Mr. Garrett taught me basic finger exercises for the right hand. With classical guitar, you pick with your fingers—not a pick. Fingerpicking would become immensely useful and a major advantage over other guitarists. When you could fingerpick, you could play music that others couldn't. He also showed me some left-hand fingerings and how to read basic music. He patted me on the back and said, "Make sure you practice—everything is in the practice." As I was leaving, he added, "Will, you're going to need another guitar! I have a student-style Yamaha I can sell you—it's not that expensive." He said it would cost two hundred dollars. I panicked. Not that expensive? That was like ten thousand dollars for a sixteen-year-old. My parents didn't have that kind of money lying around. I had to figure it out on my own—again. Ding, ding, ding—I got it. I had been into coin collecting for years. My Grandmom Milly used to give me silver dollars, and I had saved about two hundred dollars' worth of them. I never thought I'd part with them—but this felt like a great investment.

At my next lesson, I showed up with that $200 and bought the Yamaha from Mr. Coke-Bottle Eyes. I thought he was going to stroke out from excitement—I'm sure he marked it up. I absolutely loved that guitar. I played for hours on it, even fell asleep with it in my hands. It was relaxing, meditative, and something I was just naturally in tune with. After three weeks of lessons, I went up the street to Jay's to hang out. He was in his basement, and I picked up his electric guitar, which was plugged into a Fender Twin Reverb amplifier—a premier amp in 1979. I started fingerpicking a tune I had just learned, and Jay almost fell out of his chair. He couldn't believe it. I had only been playing three weeks—he'd been playing three years—and he couldn't do that. He pretty much quit shortly after that, and somehow, I wound up with his guitar and amp too. With multiple instruments, I was having a blast—totally in my zone of vibrational harmony.

In my mind, I always called music the universal language. When you played an instrument, you connected with it. It grounded you vibrationally and spiritually to the Earth. One thing I believed you could see in most musicians, whether professional or not, was peace in their soul when they played. Even if their lives were a mess offstage, when they played music, they were happy and grounded. By eighteen, I considered myself an accomplished guitarist. One day I went down to Philadelphia to a famous local music store to buy a new guitar. The owner, Bernie, was an older guy who loved to wheel and deal with locals and famous musicians alike. Bernie was well-known nationwide for great deals. I'd had a few electric guitars over time, but none felt quite right. While there, I looked up at the guitars hanging from the ceiling—and saw the most beautiful one I'd ever seen. A gold Fender Stratocaster. It had a gold body, gold hardware, and a white pickguard. It was stunning. It was a reissue from the 1960s limited edition. Price tag: $500. I thought it was a steal. I bought it, brought it home, plugged it into the Fender Twin Reverb—and it sounded and played so sweet. Even the case was awesome—gold tweed.

Unfortunately, about a week later, I got into a car accident in my restored 1950 black Chevy fastback that my Grandpop Pat had given me. It was a tragedy after all those years of restoring that car. I had to sell the gold Fender to buy a cheap car just to get to work. That whole event crushed me. A month later, I went back and bought another gold Fender Strat—but it didn't feel quite the same. I really think the first one was slightly better. It was rare. I had only ever seen Eric Clapton and a few others play one on stage.

After discovering the energy and power of the electric guitar, I stopped going to my classical guitar lessons of two years and never saw Mr. Garrett again. For me, it was all about rock 'n' roll. The love of guitar was imprinted on me forever. It led me to great creativity in both playing and writing. With that gold Fender Strat, I thought I was headed to rock and roll stardom. Later, that guitar would be part of a night I would never forget—one that had nothing to do with playing music, but everything to do with that gold guitar and something far more profound.

MUSIC IS THE SOUL'S OWN SPEECH

Throughout history, music and the fundamentals behind music have been a driving force that greatly affected mankind and me very deeply. Music was a language, a feeling, and a personal expression for musicians. For me, music was connected to a higher vibrational place, either conscious or subconscious, for all those who could see or feel it in that form. All forms of music had roots going way back to ancient times. Even over the past several hundred years, I felt that only a handful of musicians had truly been able to connect on an extremely high spiritual level. It was hard to say if those great musicians who used the power that music provided to connect spiritually did so intentionally or not.

Some great musicians I began to reflect upon when I was still a teenager were: on piano, Vladimir Horowitz; on cello, Yo-Yo Ma; and on guitar, Jimi Hendrix. What set those musicians apart from others was not just the fact that they were great musicians, it was how they connected with the higher self through music and shared it with us. When you watched them play, that spiritual connection was unmistakable. They didn't just play the music—they were the music. Their higher spiritual self was expressed through them entirely when they played. Every fiber of their being, down to a cellular level, was vibrationally connected with the Earth and Universe. Those great vibrational forces of a higher spiritual self were very evident to me as they played their instruments. You could read it in their body language, facial expressions, and overall being. They allowed themselves to be a vessel for those vibrational forces. There have always been many great musicians throughout history, and in many instances, they may have been considered technically better than the ones I admired. The difference was that they were either just technically great, or they only connected spiritually here and there, if at all. They were not completely vibrationally connected like the great musicians were. It was one thing to play technically and mathematically, but another thing altogether to play from the soul and a higher self. A perfect example of that was my own impressions of great guitar players.

For most of my early guitar-playing years, I had considered Jimi Hendrix to be revolutionary for his time, but that was about it. I honestly did not have a lot of respect for him as a great guitar player. I thought he was quite overrated. He seemed to me just to be a guy super high on drugs most of the time, doing some cool innovative things ahead of his time—but that was it. I was very wrong. I began to take a deep dive into not only his history and playing, but I also absorbed any information I could find on him at the time. Somehow, I missed it—but there it was, right in front of me. When you watched Jimi play, he was one of the greats for sure, and he was completely connected spiritually with the music. I even felt he may have been one of the great spiritual people in our history, as crazy as that might sound to some. After learning what a great spiritual person he was—and a kind, loving, and incredibly talented human being—I could have nothing but the utmost respect for him and honestly be in awe of his abilities. Yes, other guitar players could play the notes and be technically better, but they did not connect on that total spiritual level or even come close to Jimi. I really can't think of another single guitar player who did it that completely. Hendrix played with every cell in his body and let the force come through him when he played. Amazingly, I heard that he could play both left-handed and right-handed and was even seen playing things backward on the spot. It really didn't matter how the music or the instrument presented itself, he was fully in touch with it and could play the guitar any way he wanted to.

To me, music certainly was the universal language that crossed all boundaries, and I personally felt it could vibrationally connect all beings—if they were open to it. You could go into any old-age home and witness older men and women who had been inactive for quite a long time, and music would awaken something inside of them. They may have even been deeply depressed, but if you played a piece of music from their lifetime, when they were younger, you would see the light come back into their eyes. They would light up and smile with joy—or sometimes sadness—when they heard the music. I also believed that music had the ability to attach to our memories throughout our own personal history—major events, falling in love, the first kiss, the death of a loved one, or whatever it might be. I knew for sure that there was a song that could take you to that point in your life. What a beautiful, magical gift music was to all of us. It frustrated me that music was constantly being attacked in school districts across our country. It was widely known that music helped children and adults at all levels. Music increased reading capabilities, helped with math, and even had a calming influence on people's lives. Most of us had blurted out at some point, "Oh my God, how do people listen to that type of music?"—including myself—or "This new music today is terrible, it's trash," et cetera. Although we were not meant to gravitate toward all forms of music, the fundamentals beneath all styles of music were the same. I felt strongly that it was also true that connecting to a higher place through music was not always connected with a good place. You could just as easily connect with a darker force from beyond, if so desired.

The two types of music where I could see people let go and spiritually connect with it the most were gospel and some other forms of heavy metal and death metal. I also didn't feel that all hard rock or metal music connected with a dark side. In fact, I loved a lot of hard rock and heavy metal music myself, especially since I was a guitar player. There were, certainly, certain forms of music, though, that dove into the dark side. I recognized that both gospel and heavy, dark types of music had an extremely high energy level—especially when you witnessed them live. Some of the greatest vocalists on the planet were from gospel music, and I believed it was because they sang from different depths, into those higher spiritual places that they fully believed in. Gospel singers completely committed to the music with their whole heart and soul, and it allowed them to be amazing vocalists. The same could be said for the darker metal music too. The energy there—and the guitar playing—was off the charts because of their connection to the forces that they too totally believed in. Both completely contrasting styles of musicians and vocalists allowed the energy to run through their entire vibrational being.

I believed that we were all capable of those deep vibrational musical connections, but some of us were just truly exceptional at it. My spirit believed that sound was a gift to all of us and a wonderful tool to connect with our higher self. There was literally music all around us every day, at every given moment, through the sounds that we created—or that nature had created for us. My deeper self-awareness could easily see that the forest, oceans, and skies were full of music, for those who chose to hear and embrace it. In my mind, I summed it all up with a beautiful old saying that went as follows: For heights and depths no words can reach, music is the soul's own speech.

6

SHIFTING TIDES

Along with my teenage musical explorations, great shifts were occurring simultaneously in my life. Just like water flowing in a stream passes a location only once, so too were the days of my maturing life. The only exceptions for this old Scorpio soul were occasional glimpses ahead in time or reflections back to ancient times. Great tidal shifts were occurring in my world that I had to learn to navigate. For a long period in my younger years, things for me were pretty much what some would call normal. Other than being an intense creative kid, I didn't really think much about how different I truly was. Then, as my mid-to-late teen years unfolded, suddenly the dynamics of my childhood began to change. That little boy Will was becoming a young man.

Life went from fishing and going to the playground to play various sports with my friends, to what I thought of as a dead period in my life. In one respect, life was exciting and new because I had finally reached the legal driving age of sixteen, but other more familiar parts began to sadly fade. Driving a car opened all new possibilities and adventures for me and some of my friends, because we were no longer trapped in our neighborhood or limited to how far a bicycle could take us. That time also marked the start of the disconnection of our childhood crew, and I hated it. We all started venturing out to meet other people in other neighborhoods and at work. Then my friend Jay moved away—about a half hour from us—but to me, that seemed like an eternity. I really missed him, and my other friends and I would drive to see him here and there. The day-to-day hanging out was over, and it was something I missed terribly. Jay was no longer at my back door ringing the black metal bell for me to come out and play. We were becoming young men and moving on with the natural flow of life. I often had a deep nagging feeling and wondered if I had done enough and was there enough for my family and friends.

One day, when I was sixteen, I had a very strange and confusing event while driving my car. The odd occurrence wasn't because I was a new driver or using alcohol or drugs—at that point, I was a health freak and did not put any alcohol or drugs into my body. I was driving through a town not far from where I grew up, near a well-known local mall. Within the blink of an eye, I found myself several towns away on a completely different road! I had absolutely no explanation for the event, but it left me totally confused. I didn't black out and suddenly went driving that distance without realizing it. I began gathering as much research as I could on those types of events. I found out that similar things had happened to pilots over the years while flying. Suddenly, they too would end up in a completely different area in an instant. There was no real explanation for these strange occurrences, and often the pilots were blamed for blacking out. I felt it was quite possible our reality was somehow vibrationally manipulated or that we accidentally drifted into some sort of alternate dimension temporarily. It may sound farfetched—but so was the legend of the silverback gorilla until it was finally discovered in 1902. There is so much we don't know or understand just within our own world here, so how could we possibly comprehend all that lies beyond? My mysterious driving event imprinted on my mind and was just the beginning of other strange events that would unfold before me on my young journey.

From a spiritual point of view, I was still heavily entrenched in my childhood Catholic upbringing—yes, mass every Sunday and twelve years of Catholic school indoctrination. In fact, in my late teens, I was going to Catholic mass every day in my church's chapel at 6:30 am. At that time, I was really looking for a deeper sense of higher spirituality and connection to everything around me. I certainly did not find what I was looking for in that little chapel, filled mostly with a bunch of old people. It felt like we were just spilling out mindless responses to the prayers that we were trained like dogs to respond to on cue, with little meaning behind it whatsoever. Somewhere deep within me, I felt there was more intense and deeper meaning to the universe, God, and the world around us. Yes, I had my own personal vibrational awareness of life, but I was young and did not fully understand it all. I craved more spiritual knowledge and a much deeper understanding. I did eventually get a glimpse that year, when I was sixteen and a junior in high school.

I attended the local Catholic high school, Bishop Egan for boys. It was a great school compared to the local public schools, but it had its own chaotic and unbalanced vibe. Truthfully, splitting the boys and girls into separate schools was insane. It only created more havoc because the girls were not there to balance the boys' behavior. Seriously, more vulgarity flowed from our mouths to the teachers and administrators than ever would have happened if girls were in the school. Having girls there would have toned us down for sure. The theory that teenage hormones created nothing but sexual thoughts leading to a lack of quality learning was ridiculous and absolute stupidity. It only inflamed the aggressiveness and sexual drives within all of us teenagers. In my high school, we were mostly taught by Franciscan priests and brothers, along with a few lay teachers. The Franciscans were an old theological order within the Catholic Church whose ministry was mostly education. There were a lot of smart guys in that order, but they were a weird group of men. I wouldn't have let half of them around younger children ever.

That school year, it was mandatory to attend a retreat at the Franciscans' monastery, right next to the high school. The retreat was held in the evening after hours on a weekend. The purpose was for the students to connect on a deeper level with our inner spirituality, God, and our life force. Those were the things never taught in school or at church, but they were part of the founding principles within the Catholic Church. Most Catholics were served just the basic religious philosophy: do this and don't do that, and you'll go to heaven or hell—because the mass following couldn't really comprehend anything deeper. They dumbed it down for everybody, hoping the flock would stay. Oh, and let's not forget, everyone had to donate money too! The retreat was meant to dig deeper, and I was looking forward to it immensely. We were told to meditate and take quiet time to connect with our inner self and God. I'm pretty sure everyone other than me fell asleep or rolled their eyes. I could tell most kids just checked out mentally because they didn't understand it. I, however, was all in on the concept because that was exactly what I was searching for spiritually. Unfortunately, it was a short experiment and after the retreat, the Franciscans never offered it again. I was deeply disappointed and craved an even more fulfilling connection with all that was around me. I felt the Catholic Church really let me down with their watered-down doctrine they served up to followers. I was not like everyone else—I needed more and a deeper spiritual connection overall.

Not long after the retreat, I stopped going to church daily and realized it was an absolute waste of my time. Not much else happened spiritually until later down the road on my journey. I grew my hair long, popped on some flip-flops, and dove headfirst into the local rock 'n' roll scene. It was pretty much all I could think about day and night. I had been given just a glimpse of what I was searching for in that retreat, and then it was gone—but not forgotten by young Will Storz.

7

COMPUTER HIPPIE

Rounding out my high school years were pretty much boring and uneventful. I kind of fit in with every group but didn't totally fit in with any specific group. I didn't particularly care about any clique or anybody for that matter in high school. I was truly a creature unto myself and a lone wolf in many ways. I was very much a complete mystery to my fellow students as well. I wasn't an outcast, but my classmates just couldn't categorize me. I comfortably remained quiet in the background throughout my high school days. Occasionally, I would crack a joke in class or totally surprise my fellow classmates with something I did, but they could never figure me out. It was just where a Scorpio like me wanted to be — keeping them all guessing. My true loyalty remained with my childhood friends at home. I let them know me a little better but not completely. I was like the old timers would say, a mysterious onion, many layers for sure.

I graduated from high school young, at seventeen years old, and wound up with a free ride to Penn State. The free ride was not because of any great academic achievement by me, by any means, but was a result of me basically being legally considered on my own by the state. I was never really adopted by my foster parents because my real mother would never sign off. I always felt it was very spiteful on her part because she probably could not accept her own failures in life. Because of that, the state only recognized Will Campbell, not Will Storz. I also had to once again use my legal name, Will Campbell. I wasn't uncomfortable using my real name anymore, so I embraced it instead. Soon I was off to college with no clue or plan and, quite honestly, I didn't have much motivation to go into college. I was bad at math, but I was decent at writing. I never even had to do a first draft on anything. I wrote every paper off the top of my head, submitted it, and usually received an A. After a year of floundering at Penn State, I got up in class one day and walked out and never went back. I just felt like I was wasting my time and absolutely had no direction or clue what I wanted to do with my life. I was just too young to be in college at that time.

Of course, like all young aspiring rock 'n' roll stars, I wanted to make it in the music business, but I had to support myself on the side with a variety of jobs. I pretty much did anything coming down the pike. I was never afraid to work, and my dad's words were always ringing in my ears, "If you're going to do a job, do it right, even if you are working at McDonald's." He said, "Be the best burger flipper in the area, and take pride in your work, because everything leads to the next thing." I was smart enough to recognize this, but I really needed some serious direction in my life.

I decided to take a trip to Washington with a girl I was dating at the time. We went to the Smithsonian Institute and other famous places around Washington, D.C. My real purpose for going on this trip was to get my head together and figure out what I was going to do with my future, from a career standpoint, other than music. I knew that making serious money in music was a long shot and you could not stand on your own two feet for the most part; hence the term, starving musician. While I was sleeping, I had a dream, and a glowing being came to me. I could feel her intense vibrational energy, and she said, "I am Brigid, the goddess of wisdom." Then, through an illuminating mist, she gave me a glimpse of the future. I could see that the computer age was in its infancy and was just starting to really come into play in mainstream society. When I awoke, I remembered the dream and recognized the computer field as a strong, up-and-coming possible career for me.

When I returned home, I enrolled in a fast-track computer science school that was teaching computer technology at that time. My training was a mixed bag of programming, hardware, and various electronic and circuitry repairs. At that time, many of those things crossed over and were not so specialized. To get admitted to the school, I had to take an entrance exam, and as I sat in the waiting room, I watched one guy after another come out with their heads hanging low because they had failed the entrance exam and were not accepted into the school. So, my time came to take the test, and quite honestly, I never tested well in the past because I was very slow and methodical. Eventually, the moderator who ran the test came out and said to me, "Under normal circumstances, you would have failed the test and not been accepted into the program." But then he said, "Will, we've made a special exception for you." He informed me that even though I didn't finish everything, I achieved such a high percentage of correct answers that they decided to extend to me the opportunity to enroll! This was a monumental breakthrough for me, and I felt like dancing in my car about my new school all the way back home. I achieved that one hundred percent on my own. It was my thought to do it, and I pursued it and captured that great small victory; suddenly I was on a path to my new career! I still had to support myself financially and pay for schooling because this time around nothing was going to be free; I had to pay for everything myself. My dad did some networking and came up with a night job for me with UPS. He had a friend who was a boss there, and my dad vouched for me. They hired me on the spot to work nights loading trucks so I could attend school during the day.

At the same time, I was a competitive bodybuilder while going to computer school during the day and working at night. I had always been focused on being in tremendous physical condition since I was twelve years old. My dad, Ed, introduced me to the original Charles Atlas workout routine that was popularized in the 1920s. That routine was based on isometric exercises, which were all exercises performed with just your own body's resistance. Later, I moved into traditional weightlifting and bodybuilding. Being in great physical condition was always a part of who I was. I always believed that our physical beings needed to be respected and kept in the greatest condition possible. I felt that both our physical and spiritual self-development needed to be in perfect vibrational harmony. I was always exhausted from getting very little sleep. Something had to give, so I gave up my bodybuilding life. I had made the right decision; I focused everything on school and eventually graduated.

The computer school had a placement program, and businesses would come in and hire us right out of school based on our skills and credentials. I finally received an offer from a company called Positron. They were going to first train me on their computer systems for a short period. Then I was going to fly around the country and install their systems; teach the new clients how to use them and do some inspections and some software work. I accepted the job and went in and told UPS that I was leaving and gave them my two-week notice. I, Will Campbell, was extremely proud, and with that, I began my exciting new computer career.

My work in the computer field was simply awesome; I wouldn't have traded it for anything. I took a jet to work around the country every few days, and I visited practically every state in our great United States of America. I was able to see so many beautiful parts of our country that most people never had a chance to experience. I had the opportunity of meeting many people across our great country and communicating with them on all different levels; quite simply, I loved my job. I had total freedom in my new career, and most of all, I had respect from others in my field. My travels in the computer field were vast, and I was one of four people in the company of over two hundred and fifty employees who were basically allowed to dress however we wanted. I could wear my hair however I wanted and dress however I wanted too as well. If I completed my assigned job on time, the company would give me freedom in return. I was naturally great interacting with clients and their staff. All four of us guys who traveled were a wee bit eccentric, and I was no exception. I had long blonde hair, still rocking the flip-flops, and kind of dressed like a hippie rock 'n' roll dude. But I knew my job, and I was always professional. I also had to learn how to interact with contractors twice my age on the job sites. I had to inspect their electrical work, and quite often they were almost always wrong. I had to school them in the correct way to set up the wiring for our computer systems and do it in a way that didn't offend them. I had a knack for communicating well with those electrical contractors and getting them to see it my way; even though I was just a kid in my twenties. The difference between me and the other three guys with my position was that the computer field was not only their job, but it was also their hobby too. It was not my hobby, even though I loved it and was very good at it. Truthfully, my goal was to get the job done perfectly, efficiently, and enjoy myself. I always started by inspecting the electrical and signal cable wiring on the sites, then I installed the Point-of-Sale computer systems. After that, I spent a few days training the staff on how to use the systems. Then, I trained management on how to use their end of it, including inventory, bookkeeping, etc. I did a lot of custom programming for the clients while on the road as well. Basically, I just stayed up for many hours, sometimes over two or three days straight in front of a computer terminal programming. I would have food and coffee brought to me until I knocked out all the custom software for them. Once I was in my zone with work, I did not want to be disturbed until I completed it. If the other three guys around the country who did my job finished their work, they would go play in their hotel rooms on their computers, but I had a different agenda. This is how it pretty much went for me: finishing the job right and as efficiently as I could for the client and then getting a good drink and listening to some good live music. Then most importantly to the old Scorpio in me was, I needed to find a beautiful woman to share my free time with.

Not much was happening with me during that time in the spiritual realm, other than some nights when some sort of presence would press down on me while I was attempting to sleep. That sort of thing happened to me various times throughout my life, and sometimes it was hard to tell what that actual presence was. They didn't always reveal themselves as a presence for something good or something bad. For the most part, I was awake and frozen and couldn't move any part of my body, but I could feel it over me. More than half of the medical field believed there was a medical explanation for this phenomenon. They said people were just trapped in a sleep pattern called sleep paralysis. The medical field said people just thought they were awake. Well, I disagreed completely because I was fully aware enough of my body and mind to know the difference. For the most part, an occasional presence over me was about all I had on a deep vibrational level within me. I thought of it as a spiritual quiet period in my life. I had an exciting career, and I was blessed with the opportunity to visit many fantastic places all over this great country, but one night would be vastly different for me. It was a night that I would never forget, and a night that would haunt me for many years to follow.

TERROR IN THE NIGHT

While on one of my regular business trips to Missouri during my computer days, I encountered a job that seemed much like most others—or so I thought at the time. I always found it exciting to visit new places across the country. I loved the diversity of people and the unique cultural vibes in every state I visited. Yet something about this new location's energy felt unusually off to me and I couldn't quite put my finger on why.

I arrived at the customer's store—a Hardee's restaurant— and began work as usual. The first item on my schedule was to conduct electrical inspections, followed by checking if the computer inventory had shipped to the site, so I could begin installation. The installation went smoothly, and then I moved on to customizing the customer's database. This involved uploading all the necessary onsite software. As usual, I sat at the computer terminal and started the data entry, determined not to leave until the job was done, even if it meant eating and drinking right there for hours. In the end, I stayed awake for nearly two days straight, pushing myself to exhaustion. Once finished, I headed to my small motel nestled along the Missouri River—the Huck Finn Motel. Little did I know how deeply that night would be etched in my memory forever.

Late that night, when I finally entered my room at the Huck Finn Motel, I was ready to collapse and catch some desperately needed sleep. Exhausted, I went straight to bed and fell immediately asleep. But a few hours later, everything changed. I began sensing a deep, negative vibrational energy rising around me. Suddenly, I was jolted awake, horrified. Slowly, I became aware of someone on top of me, their hands pressing against my chest. Confused and disoriented, I tried to understand what was happening, but having been so exhausted, I had no idea where the door or window was—only complete darkness and a person above me with hands on my chest.

Things worsened quickly as their hands slid from my chest up to my neck, then slowly, increasing pressure. I somehow kept processing everything yet remained completely still. Oddly, though my instinct when startled is to fight back, I didn't react. Something deep inside urged me to stay silent and still—a protective mechanism, I suppose—and I trusted it. I feared I might die and wasn't sure what else to do. Eventually, the pressure around my neck eased. I was terrified but still felt the person's presence hovering over me. They moved away from the bed but stayed in the room. My heart pounded so loudly I worried they could hear it along with my breathing.

I struggled to stay calm despite being at a severe disadvantage—totally in the dark and unfamiliar with my surroundings. I assumed I was being robbed or perhaps something worse. This ordeal stretched on for hours, or at least it felt like endless terrifying hours. Periodically, the person returned to lean over me as if checking on me. I remained utterly silent, unsure if they thought they had killed me or what, but I wouldn't risk moving. Suddenly, a glowing being appeared in my mind and calmed me. He said his name was Belleek and that he was my guardian. He promised to protect me and instructed me to stay still and calm. I felt I knew him from long ago and trusted him completely, so I obeyed. I never heard anyone leave, but eventually, sunlight began to filter through the window, faintly illuminating the room.

Seeing what appeared to be a door, I sprang up and bolted toward it, opening it quickly and rushing out. After waiting a while, I returned to check my belongings—all intact. Nothing was taken. I was dumbfounded by what had happened and couldn't make sense of it. There was no evidence that anyone had been there, yet I knew better. I didn't call the police; I just wanted to leave. At the front desk, the manager asked how my stay was. "Are you kidding me?" I replied sharply, then threw my room key at him and left. With two more days of work ahead, I drove a good distance to stay at a large, fancy Holiday Inn.

In my new room, I barricaded myself with everything I could. I tried to recall every detail from the night before. I noticed an adjoining door to another room and suspected that might have been how the person entered. There were no marks on my body, but the scars of terror were forever etched on my mind.

I revisited that night again in my mind many times. I eventually concluded that perhaps no actual person had been in the room with me at all, but some kind of negative entity. Whatever it was, it was certainly not benign. Maybe the room had once been the site of a murder or some tragic event. Negative energy from such tragedies can linger for centuries, affecting the living long after. Through further research, I found many similar accounts from around the country—clearly, I was not alone in experiencing something like this. One thing was certain: whatever happened that night stayed with me forever, marking one of the most terrifying moments of my life. But as fate would have it, other strange, unsettling events awaited me in the future.

8

THE TIME TRAVELER

By my late twenties, I sadly lost my grandpop Pat McAlinden at the age of 86. After surviving a stroke, he eventually passed away from heart failure. About a year and a half later, my grandmom, Milly McAlinden, also passed away at the age of 83, after a long battle with Alzheimer's disease. I also was ready to settle down from my wild and carefree days. I began dating a young woman named Raelene. We met at a ski house that some friends and I were renting for the winter season. During one of the many parties there, we instantly had great natural chemistry, and young love quickly blossomed. I was blessed to also meet her wonderful parents. Her mother's name was Polly, and her father's name was Mac. Polly was a very spiritually intuitive woman, and Mac was the complete opposite; he was an aerospace engineer and very scientifically driven. After about a year and a half, we tied the knot and joined together in marriage. Not long after, we purchased our first home and began a new journey together.

Raelene was very vibrationally sensitive as well, it came from her mother's side of the family. As a young girl, she would get overwhelmed by the vibrations of various sounds, like a dripping faucet. She said her mother Polly could see auras and was extremely intuitive too. When Raelene was young, her mother would put Uno cards on her belly, then place Raelene's hand on them to guess the colors and numbers. Those capabilities stayed with her, and as a young woman, I even watched her know every card in a poker deck just by touching it. Over time, she seemed to push a lot of those feelings away. I suppose it was all a bit too intense for her, but she would lean on her capabilities occasionally from time to time. Like many young couples, we enjoyed life and headed down our own wonderful joint journey together. As a young couple, we spent a lot of time with friends and family. We also had many side hustles for extra cash, and we were natural-born entrepreneurs. One of our side gigs led us to an evening that slowly unfolded with an incredible meeting of someone who would profoundly imprint upon me forever.

Raelene and I were always looking to make an extra buck, so we decided to take some side work for her brother Mike, who ran a security guard company. I always liked Mike a lot; then he offered me some security night work, driving around in my vehicle to different store and warehouse locations. I accepted the first job that Mike offered. I had to go to a warehouse after hours, check in at the guard house, and make rounds in the warehouse every hour to make sure all was secure in the building. When I arrived the first evening, I parked my car and headed into the warehouse. It was a massive open space with some offices on the perimeter of the main open area. The guard shack was about seventy-five yards in the center of the open warehouse. As I was heading to the guard shack, I immediately felt a deep uneasiness within me. Something about that place did not feel right. I made my first rounds and things went okay, but it was very creepy and unsettling. I then went back to the guard shack for a short break before my next rounds. Suddenly, I heard loud bangs across the warehouse. When I went to investigate the sounds, I found several large fifty-five-gallon steel drums knocked over and laying on the floor. When I had done my first rounds, they were all standing upright! No one was there but me, so I became a bit freaked out. The steel drums were very heavy and could not possibly fall over on their own. I decided to do my second rounds to be sure no one was in the building. On my second walk, in one of the side rooms, I noticed a large ball of wrapped heavy plastic rolled up in the middle of the room. It was probably about eight feet in diameter. After I finished that set of rounds, I headed back to the guard shack for another short break. It was now after midnight when I headed out for my third set of rounds. When I approached the room where the giant roll of plastic was, I could not believe what I saw. The giant ball of rolled-up plastic was now out in a big hallway outside the room it had previously been in! There was only a normal three-foot-wide doorway to that room. I thought, "How was that possible?" The plastic ball could not fit through the doorway, and I had not heard any sounds at all prior to its haunting move. Once again, I felt a bad presence in the building, and I was not comfortable staying in there. I immediately left and finished the night in my car outside. I refused to ever go back there again, and the next day I told Mike to see if there was some other job he could send me to. I told him what had happened, and he laughed and said that other guards would not take that job either. Mike said he would find me another assignment, and I was relieved.

Mike finally called with another job for both Raelene and me. We were assigned to just drive through the parking lots of clients and make sure that there was nothing going on, like vandalism around the stores late at night into the wee hours of the morning. As it turned out, the stores were not all in great locations around Philadelphia. Some of the areas that we patrolled were considered pretty sketchy. Well, money always talked, so we took the gig. At some point, we got lost going to our last location and wound up in a rough neighborhood. It was before the days of cell phones and our wonderful modern technology. I was getting increasingly frustrated and nervous about driving in those areas late at night, just the two of us. So, we decided to pull the car over and find a pay phone to talk to the guy that we were supposed to relieve, to get better directions. Right before the call, I was extremely frustrated at being lost in that rough location, and I was not using the best language when referring to that wonderful area that we were lost in that late at night. I finally made the call and talked to a guy named Vince. He sounded very articulate over the phone, and he told us to relax, and he proceeded to give us good directions. We finally made it to the correct location—late, but safe and sound—thanks to Vince. As I was looking for Vince, and right as we got out of my Chevy Monte Carlo, walking toward me was this skinny, older, short, gray-haired African American man. The first thing he said to me was, "Hi, I'm Vince. Bet you didn't expect a skinny old black dude who speaks well." He then made another comment about my colorful vocabulary that I was using just prior to arriving there. We were quite surprised that he knew what I had said. Then suddenly he just froze where he was, standing about five feet away from me.

He then began telling us information about both of us—personal information that he could not have ever known. Vince became particularly locked onto me; he even told me that I had my gold electric Fender Stratocaster guitar in my trunk, and sure enough, that guitar was in the trunk! I was fascinated by the unfolding event, and he said to me, "I have a strong connection with you because we grew up the same. We are old souls from long ago." He continued to spout off a lot of the things that he knew about us, and he said, "I know about these things because of what happened to me when I was a child and that me and him came from very similar backgrounds." Vince said, "I came from a Catholic orphanage just like you did, but while I was there, when I was a little kid, I was always hungry. The nuns there used to put out some bread with strychnine poisoning on it to kill the rats." He said that he remembered waking up on a cold table and removing the cover that was over him, and he could also see a door with a small window up top. He went over to the door and looked out the window. Eventually, somebody came by on the opposite side of the door and started freaking out and began screaming and yelling. Well, as it turned out, little Vince was in a morgue, and he woke up! He apparently had eaten the bread with strychnine poisoning on it and was pronounced dead, but somehow, he came back to life! When he came back, he said things were different, and he had a great insight into life, the afterlife, and an incredible sense of intuition. He said to me that a glowing being told him that it was not his time yet and that he had more to do on his journey. Vince understood a lot of things that most people could never comprehend due to that incredible event that took place in his young life. Vince said that he could feel a common energy between me and him, and that's why he connected with me so much. I was completely amazed by his incredible story.

Raelene and I spent hours listening to him that evening. He stayed and just talked to us about life, intuition, and a sense of knowing beyond what is normal to most people. He also went into tremendous detail about death and what happens after we die. I had never heard anything like that up to that point in my life, he was very specific about everything too. Truthfully, I could not remember every detail, but it was extremely overwhelming yet fascinating at the same time. Vince had told us that death or passing is a process, and that we go through several layers. Some people get stuck at different layers for various reasons, and some move on, but it was much more specific than that. There was just so much information that he spewed out that it was very hard to comprehend it all at that time. Amazingly, all that information came from a guy that looked practically homeless and by no means would've appeared to have that kind of knowledge. I was so wrong about my preconceptions of him, and I had a lot to learn for sure. I didn't want the night to end; it was really that profound. Eventually, morning came, and we unfortunately had to part ways.

Sadly, I was only ever able to see Vince one more time in my life, and that was not too long after our first meeting. I met him for the second time at a restaurant, and we sat down and talked a bit more about life and various deep, profound issues. Vince did not consider himself psychic in terms that most people know. In fact, he was quite shy and bothered by anybody asking him to do a reading or anything of that sort. He did not view himself in that way at all. He was deeply vibrationally connected to all that was around him, including the Earth and the Universe. Vince was not some fake carnival psychic preying on desperate people for money. He was the real deal, and if you ever met someone like that, you would know the difference—

no mistake about it. Vince said that he had something very important to tell me. He told me that Mercury was one of the glowing ones from long ago that sent him to me. Mercury was the god of messaging and time travel who sent Vince on his journeys through different lives. They guided him toward people and different jobs for whatever reason—to touch those people in need of guidance. At that point, he was a security guard; another time he might be working as a healthcare worker, or whatever was needed of him. He said he was here for me to help me understand a deeper awakening that would soon be coming to me.

Vince and I had a deep, ancient vibrational connection, and then just like that, he was gone forever. I longed for another meeting with him, but it would never come. Vince was a truly remarkable person. I was very thankful for the opportunity and the knowledge that he passed onto me. I believed that we were destined to meet for sure. There was a lot that he told me that would take many years for me to fully understand. Vince the time traveler was an absolute gift to me, and he helped open my mind even more to the deep, underlying vibrational connections between all of us.

9

GLOWING ONES

I was now in my late twenties and no longer working on the road with my computer job around the country. The traveling around the country had just burned me out, so I accepted a local technician's position at the same company. My new position allowed me to be closer to home, but it was a step backwards in my career. I was now just one of many technicians, and my territory was the Philadelphia and New Jersey region. I was on call twenty-four seven and had to always carry a beeper on me. I hated it and no longer had the freedom that I had with my previous position in that company. Raelene and I started a little side gig running karaoke shows for nightclubs. It was a new thing back then and quickly became very popular and very good side money for us. It eventually led to an extremely profound life event that made me look at myself closely for the rest of my life.

One day we received a call from another couple named Laura and Ted, who wanted to rent our equipment when we weren't using it for their own karaoke shows. I introduced myself as Will, and after chatting for a while, I agreed to the deal and over time we became friendly with the couple. Laura told us she was doing some other side work as a psychic for private parties as well. My deep inner instincts were a little skeptical of her abilities, but I remained open-minded about it. Raelene and Laura coordinated a private psychic party one evening at our little townhouse for friends. Laura showed up midway through the party, wearing a black dress and very much appearing like what people thought a psychic would look like. We dimmed the lights, and she began her presentation to the group in attendance. Laura went around to different people in the group and brought up various information about them—from their love lives to their financial situations, doing a generalized reading of everyone. It felt very carnivalesque to me, but I just went along with everything and enjoyed the evening. After our guests left, it was just me, Raelene, Laura, and Ted left in our townhouse. Laura looked over at me, gave me a sly smile, and said maybe I should've had you read me instead. She said, "I'm aware of all that Scorpio energy you're hiding over there because I'm a Scorpio too." Then Laura turned to me and said, "Would you like to do something cool?" I asked her, "Well, what is it?" Laura said, "Let's do a past life regression together. I think you may find it very interesting." I agreed to go along with her guidance, figuring it might be fascinating and cool. I had never participated in a past life regression before and was curious and very open to the new experience.

Laura asked Raelene and Ted to give us some privacy. Then Laura had me sit in a comfortable chair with the lights dimmed even more as she began the past life regression. She told me she could not make anything happen to me and was just there as a guide, and I had to be open to it. She said, "Let your body relax and notice your breathing. Stay focused on your breath and allow yourself to drift off to a peaceful calm place." She told me to slowly drift further and deeper into my subconscious self to a long time ago. I did as she instructed and let myself go completely into a deep meditative state in the regression. I could slowly feel the vibrational energy within me shifting and becoming more intense. It was strange because I was completely aware of my normal self in the room simultaneously. She asked, "What do you see?" I replied, "I see a calming white mist." Laura told me to go toward the mist and again tell her what I began to see. I told her as I passed through the mist, I saw a peaceful garden with beautiful flowers and an iron greenish bench, like the color of weathered copper. I noted that I could see someone sitting on the bench from behind it. At that point in my regression journey, I kept describing what I was feeling and seeing. From a distance, I could see a tiny glowing orb slowly moving toward me. As the orb got closer, it got bigger, and then in an instant, there was a very strange glowing type of being right in front of me. I was not afraid as the glowing being said to me, "I am Ecne, the God of Wisdom, Knowledge and Enlightenment." There were no actual words spoken, but a complete understanding between us through thought. He told me I was one of the glowing ones as well and needed to always remember my roots and help those weaker ones around me throughout my lives. One day, my journey would come full circle, and only then, after I fulfilled and completed my work, would I truly return home. He also told me that I had been given great inner strength and high intuition. He then pointed at the person sitting on the bench and said for me to look upon that face and see the future. He told me my journey may seem long, but it was merely a flash in what those on Earth call time. He ended by saying, "Never squander your gifts and soon you will return to your eternal home with us." Ecne then disappeared into the glowing orb and slowly drifted away from me. Then I moved around toward the front of the bench to observe the person sitting there as I gazed at that person's face. There was an unusual familiarity that came over me at first; I thought it was my biological father or perhaps a deceased biological grandfather of mine. However, the more I looked deeper upon that face, I realized it was really me! The man sitting on the bench was me in the future as a much older man. I was completely confused and amazed at the same time over the whole event that unfolded before me. That image instantly imprinted upon my mind, and it was an image I surely would never forget. Then I became silent for a while, while Laura began to slowly guide me out of my past life regression. I suddenly was back within my current self. We both just stared at each other, then we hugged, and I thanked her for assisting me in that profound journey back in time. We never spoke of the regression ever again.

Seeing myself as an old man was a gift and a message that I would need to reflect upon to fully comprehend over the course of my future journey in life. I walked away with a much greater sense of knowing why I felt a lot of things I had felt since I was very small. I finally understood that those deep vibrational instincts within me were there from long ago and perhaps I did have some other purpose in the current life I was blessed with. Even though I was still a young man, I felt a sense of clarity on many things within me as I moved forward down the road of life. I already knew what I would look like as a much older man too; it was uniquely strange. The remarkable glimpse into my past was one that I knew would stay with me forever.

10

MR. PIANO

After several years of me still being a slave to my beeper, I switched my job to another company very similar to the original one I worked for. It was a much larger company called Micros. I was just a technician for them and the company would not allow me to touch any of the software work. It was very frustrating having to watch their programmers even though I knew my skillset was way better than theirs. I was absolutely bored to death, and I just felt like I had taken a big step backwards in my career. I began to feel a deep vibrational shift within me. I knew that I needed a change in my life, but I was not sure what exactly that would be.

One day I had a conversation with Raelene about my non-contentment with work. She suggested that maybe I should somehow try to make money from some sort of musical source.

Maybe I could be happy with it and make a decent living too. Well, it was well known that making money from music was extremely difficult. We were a young married couple and there wasn't a lot of income coming in to begin with at that time. Raelene approached me about the idea of me becoming a piano tuner. She suggested that I call some guy that she looked up in a phone book listing about piano tuning. I said to her that I didn't know really too much about piano tuning. At best I understood pitch and how to tune a guitar by ear but that was the extent of it. I decided to give it a shot and just call the guy in the ad. I introduced myself as Will Campbell and told him that I was interested in getting into the piano tuning trade. He said unfortunately he could not help me, but at the last second he said he knew someone named Craig who might be able to help me. After he gave me his number, I wasted no time and proceeded to call the other guy, Craig. Once again, I introduced myself and then I told Craig that I was really interested in getting into the piano tuning business. I spoke with Craig for a while through some small talk, and we proceeded with a general feeling out of each other. He said, "you know, I have a good feeling about you just from over the phone." Craig said, "Why don't you come in and meet me, and we'll talk a little bit further." I thanked him and then I set up a meeting with him at the top local piano store, called Tyler's Music. Craig was the manager of the piano technicians at that piano store. At the time, I had long blonde hair down to my nipples, and I for sure looked like a dead ringer for a musician. I still dressed appropriately for the interview with him and gave him respect while speaking to him. He even commented about that; He said, "Will I appreciate that you didn't say, dude and that's cool yeah and use all that stupid mindless street vocabulary." I was very professional, not like people who didn't know how to conduct themselves in an interview. Keep in mind, I came from a good career, and I knew how to deal with other professionals. We hit it off right away, and Craig offered to train me for free. However, to do this training, I would have to do it during the day like a normal full-time job. I would also have to support myself once again through some sort of odd job.

I was able to hook up with a part time job that allowed me to grab some night work to help support Raelene and me during the transition period. Raelene was working for a temp work agency at the time, and she introduced me to them. The temp agency offered me a position with them. It was kind of an interesting job; I basically went to gas stations and taught people how to use the first credit card machines at the gas pumps. I began my new part time work at the pumps, meeting and greeting people. I explained to customers how to use those new credit card machine and they were very fascinated by the new technology. I met a lot of interesting people and got paid ten dollars an hour for my time.

My training with Craig took off quickly, and I was pretty much natural at it from the beginning. Truthfully, musical ability really had nothing to do with how well you could tune a piano or not. Tuning a piano came down to a much more fundamental deep feeling. It was an understanding of pitch, vibrations and the subtle nuances that make something sound nice, even though it may not be mathematically correct. Since I was learning to tune by ear, which was the traditional way, I picked everything up quickly. I was always in tune with vibrations and the frequencies they produced my whole life. Moving into my new piano tuning profession, just profoundly resonated with me.

There was also a girl named Kelly who trained with me at the same time, but she almost didn't make the cut. Craig would often talk to me about her lack of progress with her tuning ability. Craig was on the fence on whether to move forward with her or not. In the end, she managed to finally achieve what he felt were the proper standards for doing the job, but it was a close call for her. I liked Kelly, she was a very nice person and a great piano player as well.

Craig, on the other hand, was gearing me up to be a somewhat of a younger kind of moneymaking machine for the company. He felt like I had what it took to do that, because I was tuning fast and moving so quickly in my training. Craig was probably the fastest tuner in the country, and he told me that the people in the industry called him *Mr. Piano*. He could tune a piano in fifteen minutes, which most technicians didn't believe could ever be done. Craig had a particular skill set that was precise and fast. He recognized similar mechanics in me because I did not have a lot of wasted movements in me, just like him. Craig didn't speak to me about his background right away but as it turned out, it was incredible.

Craig was Frank Sinatra's piano technician, and he toured with him and worked for the Philadelphia Orchestra and many other concerts as well. Craig was also very well respected around the country by his peers. He was considered the fastest and best piano tuner in the country. I was proud to have him as my mentor and craved learning as much as I could from him. Craig had a brother named Stan who was an excellent piano technician as well. I worked alongside six other piano technicians too for quite some time. I was not ready for the road yet, but I was still learning a lot aside from just tuning pianos.

The repair part of the piano business was a totally different animal because there were so many types and styles of pianos over the past hundred years or so. There was so much for me to learn just on the repair end of the business. I stayed focused mostly on the tuning aspect, which was the art form of the job. Other than Craig and Stan there were only two other piano technicians who I liked in the group. There was an older gentleman who took me under his wing named Don and one other guy who could tune fast but got a lot of recalls named Alex.

The rest of the technicians were quite a bit odd. Honestly, I didn't know where they rounded up the other piano tuners from. They just seemed like a mix of guys zapped of personality and some of them had little anger issues hiding behind a lot of Bible thumping. I did not blend in with the odd piano tuners at all. I knew Stan would be my second-best guy to learn from. If anybody was going to have some of the little inside secrets about the piano tuning job, it would surely be Craig's brother Stan.

There were two other guys that worked there at the shop; one guy's name was Jim, and he was the piano rebuilder from Boston. Jim was phenomenal and he also helped write some of the books that technicians around the world had used to learn from. The other gentleman was a piano refinisher named Denny. I was always picking Jims's brain when it came to repairs and technical things. Jim was so reluctant to give up any information at all. It seemed like he was always worried about his job security, and he knew he was the man with the knowledge. I had to pry the info out of him, with some subtle clever ways.

Piano tuning was an art form, because it was not as mathematically correct as people might have thought. Craig would say, "It's like stuffing ten pounds of crap into a five-pound bag and making it work." The next main concern for

Craig to allow me to work with the clients was how quickly I could tune a piano. I had to be able to tune a piano in an hour or less. When I first started tuning pianos, I would spend literally all day just on the first twelve notes called the temperament. The skill it took to tune an entire piano in an hour was quite an enormous task. Craig could do it in fifteen minutes! I finally got the tuning within an hour. Craig said that it was the quickest anyone had ever picked it up.

He decided to release me on to the customer base and quickly set me up with a working territory. He pulled a lot of good areas away from other technicians to give it to me. He had faith that I could handle it, even though I was very young and new to the trade. I was not even uncomfortable going out to do the work in the beginning. I was confident that being a piano technician was the right fit for me. I just had a great feeling about it, and I was already good at dealing professionally with people.

The biggest hurdle I had to overcome when I was younger was gaining credibility. I was a long-haired hippie looking guy, coming up and ringing the doorbell of the piano clients. When the door opened, they would often look over my shoulder for some old blind man coming up the path, who had been doing it his whole life. The blind piano tuners really did not possess any extraordinary piano tuning skills, I worked with some, and I was not impressed. I was always very personable with the customers, and they did except me, once I tuned the pianos for them. I rarely had any recalls even though some of the other more experienced piano tuners did.

There was one customer who was a phenomenal concert pianist who played a Baldwin nine-foot concert grand piano. The first time I tuned her piano, she called and complained that she and her husband didn't think things were to their liking. So, Craig sent out my old friend Don, who had given me a lot of knowledge and took me under his wing. Don was always a straight shooter, and he knew that I was different than the other piano tuners. He would never consider covering something up if I had made any mistakes with mt tuning.

Don went out to check out the piano and he said to the clients, "Try the piano now and tell me what you think." They said, oh my we love it so much Don, thank you for coming and fixing it. Don said to them, "I didn't do anything, Will tuned it perfectly and you should not judge a book by its cover. Just because he has long hair and he's young, that does not make him an inferior piano tuner. Will is an extraordinary technician and I don't say that about everybody." It meant a lot to me that Don stuck up for me like that, because piano tuning was viewed as an older man's trade for sure. I finally gained that client's respect, and I continued to work for them for quite some time. Over time I realized that a lot of the old technicians were not that great, I had to fix their mistakes all the time.

Me and the other piano technicians also got together every Friday late in the afternoon for a meeting. Basically, we would discuss not only business but most importantly, what did we see that week as far as any problems. Our meetings were an invaluable experience for me every week, bouncing things off each other and coming up with solutions. Quite frankly, I don't believe there was another place in the country that had that type of forum. Those meetings were beyond priceless for all of us. Keep in mind that those were the days before the Internet and any online technical forums.

Craig was still handling the Philadelphia Orchestra account and one day when I was working in the shop, he told me to go in the back and tune a new white grand piano called a Weber. I would often just come in and tune a piano and ask Craig to give me his feedback on my work. I was always seeking to become more like him, because I had so much respect for his abilities within the trade. After I finished tuning that piano, I asked him to come and check my tuning. Craig played the piano, leaned into it and listened to it intently. He moaned and groaned and debated the tuning in his mind. Then he looked up at me and said, "it's really good, I don't have anything to tell you." I was really surprised but happy about what he said.

Well with that, Craig went into the office and said to his secretary, "Oh by the way, I'm sending Will down to the orchestra, knock the other guy off the job. I want him to do it; he can handle it." That was an extremely proud moment for me, because you had to be an excellent piano tuner to work for the Philadelphia Orchestra. Their standards were very high, and they would not except a slouch by any means. It was great to say that you worked for the Orchestra but then again, every client was important to me. Craig always told me to pay attention to your client's needs. Every piano's sound is different, and its response is different as well. He also told me that every client's perception of sound is very different. I never forgot that advice from Craig because it was very true. Every client's needs and feelings for their own instrument was unique and I always approached the job in that way.

Most of my early days as a piano tuner were really centered around me honing my skills and making more money for the company. Since I was trained by the fastest piano tuner in the world, that meant more money for the piano store. I was on board with that theory in the beginning, but slowly I changed my feelings towards that business concept. I began to realize that I was the one in touch with those customers and I began to develop personal relationships with them. I certainly did not feel that a fifteen- or twenty-minute tuning justified the cost or was even fair to the client. Once again, my dad's voice came ringing in my ear, "Take pride in what you do." I still tuned the pianos fast, but I stayed within what I felt was reasonable to the client. I was giving them a fair amount of time and a lot of myself the opportunity to socialize with the customers. I became friends with many of my customers over time and I really enjoyed the personal side of the job.

The owner of the music store's name was Frank Tyler. The only thing that I was thankful for with the owner, was that he gave me the opportunity to work in his store. Other than that, I really did not care for Frank that much at all. To me, he cheated a lot of his clients and treated the piano tuners poorly. I had been working there for quite a few years when things began to change with Tyler Music. After a variety of bad business deals, Frank was forced to sell the business to a larger, much older piano chain store who eventually bought out the Tyler Music company. The new owners were called Jansen 's music and for some reason they did not want to continue employment of the piano tuners. They did however keep Frank on as a salesman as part of the deal. Frank attempted to continue to run the service department and keep us locked in under an old noncompete contract. Unfortunately, nothing legally held up for him in the end. All the piano technicians had disbursed and either went to work for other stores or worked on their own. A lot of the office staff along with Craig and the other rebuilders and refinishers had moved on before the official store takeover. I never worked or interacted with them again.

After years of working at Tyler Music, I was excited and off to start my own piano tuning business. Although I would always be grateful to Craig for being my mentor, I decided that I would never work under someone else ever again. I had moved on and became better as a technician because I was now relaxed and working like I always wanted to. I allowed my instincts to become deeper and more vibrationally connected to my unique craft. I knew the change to working for myself would be a challenge but at least I would be calling all the shots. Once again, I was right where I wanted to be, free and doing exactly what I loved.

11

MY HIDDEN SECRET

I realized that in life, we all liked to think that we were completely transparent with who we were or how others perceived us. The truth was that it was almost humanly impossible to be that transparent. The careful and often subconscious filtering of our output information allowed us as humans to adapt and give what we felt was the best answer or no answer at all as a protective mechanism. Even me, Mr. Will Campbell, just like everyone else, had to filter information for my own personal protection. I had a rather large secret regarding my piano tuning career, that only a handful of people close to me knew about and certainly not any of my clients. It was a secret that changed me forever.

While I was still in the early part of my piano tuning career, things were going quite smoothly with my everyday work. I absolutely loved what I was doing for a living. Even though I was young at that point in my life, I felt that I was a good piano tuner and very confident in my abilities. Like any other young guy at that stage in my life, I was very active and involved with friends and adventures. One day one of my friends invited Raelene and I on a trip that they were putting together, white water rafting in West Virginia. The trip was to a place called the Gorge or Snake River whitewater rafting. Those rivers were intermediate class rapids, and they were quite intense as I was told. I was never much of a thrill seeker in my life, but it sounded like a fun outing with all my friends for the weekend, so we were happy to join the crew.

We all carpooled down in several vehicles and as we finally got into the West Virginia area, I started to feel like I was slipping back in time. We were deep in the back woods and honestly it looked like not much had changed there in many years. We had pre-arranged lodging at some campsite with cabins. We all arrived late in the afternoon and proceeded to check out the little old campsite. When we finally went to check in, we came across a young girl who greeted us. In a slow, very drawn-out old style West Virginian voice the girl said, "let me get my Maw." We kind of all looked at each other and laughed a bit off to the side; I felt like we rolled back into the 1800s. Maw finally came around with all six teeth and got us all checked in. The cabins were quite rough, and the bedding was minimal at best but hey it was a cabin, what did we expect right? So, a few of us went to see if we could change the sleeping arrangements a little bit, and we decided to go talk to Maw. She was having difficulty helping us with the situation, so she looked at us and said, "let me go get Paw!" I thought wow this was unbelievable, it surely felt like we rolled back a hundred years in time for sure. Wow, it could've been the Civil War days still, we were amazed at how backwards in time that place was. The whole scene was astounding to witness! Old Paw eventually came down to assess our situation with seven fingers and all four teeth in his mouth! He did his best with the situation, but not much was changed at all. Later that evening we were all up hanging out as most young people did. We were talking and having fun and looking forward to the next day on the river. The trip was split into two days; Saturday would be a large rafting trip down one river, with groups of us in large rafts. Then Sunday would be down a separate branch of the river, with individual smaller rafts. Something felt a little off and uneasy with me deep inside and I was not sure what it was. The Saturday trip was okay, but we quickly realized that the water levels were not where they had anticipated them to be. Some people were disappointed with this, but truthfully, I did not need to see crazy dangerous rapids anyway. The less risks that were on the river, the better it was for me. I was just looking for a fun event with my friends on a beautiful river in nature. We had a party Saturday night once we all arrived back at the cabins. Eventually everyone retired for the evening, to rest for the second leg of the trip in the individual rafts on Sunday.

Early Sunday morning, we all woke up and headed to the meeting spot with our river guide. We then headed down the river for another fun-filled day of rafting. Our whole group launched off again with the guide and headed down the river. It was quickly apparent once again that the water levels were nowhere near what had been expected. Instead of having a thrilling ride down the river, we were pretty much crawling along and, in many cases, we had to stand up and pick up our rafts. We carried our rafts through the extremely shallow portions that could not even move a one-man raft. The grumbling amongst the group began again, because it was going to be a long adventure with not much white-water fun. It was at least a four-hour trip down the river and the group had really hoped for a lot more fun. Eventually the guide could really sense everybody's frustration, so he decided to make a pit stop at an area where there was a large deep pool within the river. To remedy the boredom, his idea was to have us climb up and jump off the rocks into the deep water to create a little fun along the journey. Keep in mind, for safety reasons we all had a life vest on and a crash helmet. So, one by one we began to climb up the rocks and take turns jumping only feet first, as instructed by him into the deep pool for a thrill. The cliff was at least thirty feet to forty feet high. Finally, it was my turn to jump, and although I did not need excessive thrills and did not like heights, I gave it a go on my first jump. All went well with the first jump other than the fact that when we hit the water, the hard rush of water up into our helmets that were strapped to our chins, was harsh. The rush of the water was putting a lot of pressure on everybody's neck and chin. Once again there was grumbling amongst the group about the helmets being a problem when you hit the water. Like any genius West Virginian guide, he came up with a quick solution to the complaining and moaning amongst the group. His brilliant solution was simple, remove the helmet! Well, since we were all jumping with our feet at first it did not seem to pose any great threat to us. Everyone began their second jump and one by one we took our turns climbing up and jumping again. Everybody was much happier this time around and finally there was some fun for our group.

Eventually I made my way to the top of the rock again and prepared for my second jump. I jumped off the rock with my feet first like everyone else, but when I hit the water, I felt tremendous pressure in my left ear! Suddenly I was underwater and slightly unconscious and even on the verge of drowning without anyone realizing it! A warming glow and sense of comfort came over me. While I was under the water, Dagda, my protective guardian from when I was a child, came to protect me once again. Dagda calmed me enough to refocus myself during that dangerous situation. Finally, I was able to mentally collect myself, but I was still very disorientated, and I did not realize what had happened to me. I had a sharp pain in my left ear, and I was extremely nauseous and felt like my left ear was just filled with water. I managed to get myself to the shoreline, and I started shaking my head very hard to the left to try to remove the water from my ear. Water did come out of my ear, but it still felt completely full, almost beyond full. By then, I think people started to realize that something had happened to me. They could see that I was not right, and they came over to me to help me. I didn't really remember speaking to anyone. I suppose I just told them I got hurt on the jump; I didn't really know what was wrong with me. I was in quite a bit of pain in my left ear and very concerned! Unfortunately, it was long before the days of cell phones, and I was out in the middle of nowhere, many hours deep in the backwoods of West Virginia. Our good old boy guide didn't even have a radio to even attempt to call for any type of help. I was stuck and forced to do the remainder of the trip, which was four hours down the river! I didn't remember any part of going down the rest of the river; other than being in a lot of pain. It seemed like it was an eternity but that was just the beginning of much bigger problems for me. Once we all made it down the river, it was back to the cabins and time for everyone to pack up and start the journey to drive back home from West Virginia, which was many hours. The drive seemed like it was endless and grueling for me. I was stuck in the back of a van laying down, trying to just remove myself mentally from the pain. I could not figure out why I could not get the water out of my left ear! Raelene was quite concerned about my condition and so was I. Luckily, I did not have to drive myself home.

When I arrived home, I took some painkillers and attempted to rest from the exhaustion. The nagging pain in my ear was relentless and did not go away. I tried to take a few days off from work, but I did not make any mention to my clients about what exactly had happened to me. I wasn't even sure yet what was wrong with me, and it was frustrating. Things seemed to progress and get worse quickly, and I wound up with even more pain and even more fullness in my ear. It was suggested by my family that I go see my doctor, so I set up an appointment with my primary physician. My doctor looked at my left ear and told me that it looked like I had some water in there. He informed me that I was going to have to give it time to work itself out. He also said he couldn't really see anything and sent me on my way. That was the beginning of a big disaster for me. As the days followed, things got even worse even though I'd gone back to work piano tuning. I did not mention anything to any of my clients and did my best to act normal. I thought that maybe I just needed to stay quiet and give my body time to recover. I continued to work out of necessity, but at that point I could only hear out of my right ear. Then the yellow oozing puss began to be visible coming out of my injured ear and started running down my neck. It was obvious at that point that I had an infection in my left ear, and I was extremely concerned. I returned to the doctor, and he said yes, it looked like I had a nasty infection. He also said that from the story I told him that it was not good news. Apparently, I had some swamp water in my left ear and that created a very bad infection from all the bacteria in the water. He prescribed me some eardrops to take care of the infection but after two months nothing had changed, and I suffered with it day after day. I continued to work and hoped that at some point the drops would work but they never did. My primary physician should've sent me immediately to an Ear Nose and Throat specialist. Unfortunately, he didn't, and he let his ego get in the way, which turned out to be a major problem in the long run for me. After suffering for an extended period, I eventually went to see another doctor who was an Ear Nose and Throat specialist. I gave him all the back story, and the type of ear drops that I was using. He looked in my ear and said, "I can't see anything because of the raging infection; we have to get rid of that first." He already knew that the current ear drops were not working at all. He then said, "You know I've talked to another physician who just came across something new that not many doctors know about." He told me that there were other drops that were used for the eyes; that they had recently found out seemed to help with some stubborn ear infections as well. So, he prescribed them for me, and I was hopeful that they would work. I also developed a secondary infection on the outside of my left ear that burned and itched severely. So, he prescribed a steroidal cream for that problem as well. I returned home and tried the new drops along with the steroidal cream. Every time I used any drops in my injured ear, I felt a severe burning in my ear and then all the way down into my neck. The burning was very painful to deal with, and it would literally drop me to my knees. I had to get rid of the raging infection, so I just sucked it up. Thankfully the new drops seemed to work quickly, as well as the cream for the secondary infection. In a few days, I finally got relief from the oozing out of my ear. I still had to hide what had happened to me from my clients and that things were still not right with me.

Everything overall still didn't feel right with my left ear, all the sound coming into my left ear was muffled, and I was confused about what was going on. Once again, I went back to the doctor who prescribed the eardrops that worked. I told him that the drops had worked out great, but I was not sure what was still going on in my left ear now. He then proceeded to investigate my left ear again and was able to finally see inside with the infection gone. He said to me, "The good news is that the infection has cleared up, but the bad news is that you have a massive perforation to your eardrum." He told me that minor perforations in eardrums were common and generally would heal on their own in a circular formation until the hole closes. He then said, "Will, unfortunately for you, that was not going to be the case, because the perforation was too large, and you would need surgery to fix it!" He also told me that I should've seen an ENT specialist right away. If I had not gotten that serious infection, he also believed that the eardrum would have healed on its own. Unfortunately, the extended infection caused more damage to the tissue around the perforation and made it even larger! I was extremely upset that things were not handled properly from the beginning, especially since I made a living with my ears as a piano tuner.

There was no time to waste, and I had to schedule surgery as quickly as possible. So, I proceeded to go ahead and set myself up for the surgery with a local surgeon that the ENT doctor had recommended for difficult cases. My hope was that I would have the surgery and heal up and be fine. During the pre-surgery consult, the surgeon told me that the hole in my eardrum would be closed by grafting skin from another part of my ear. He also said that I would never have my hearing back in that ear exactly like it was before! He explained that the eardrum was unique compared to other skin in your body. Even though you're able to close it with a skin graft, it's not possible to duplicate the exact texture and all the little nuances that make the eardrum the unique part of the body that it is. I was devastated, but I had to move forward with the surgery and hope for the best. I was certainly not sure how things would go with my beloved piano tuning career moving forward at that point.

The surgery was set up quickly and when I went in the day of the surgery, everything was a success after several hours under the knife. I had to take more time off from work because my head was bandaged, and I couldn't walk around like that as a piano tuner. Eventually all the bandages came off, and I had to baby my ear for quite some time and be careful until it fully healed. I kept my clients in the dark once again, because I needed to make a living. Piano work was all that I wanted to do with my life. I really felt like I was way too deep into my new career, and I did not want to go back to the computer field again. I also completely loved what I was doing with all my heart and soul. The hearing in my left ear for sure was not one hundred percent. There was a noticeable difference even when it came to listening to music or trying to sing and play a piano or guitar at the same time. Things were clearly different, and they were never going to be one hundred percent again.

For some reason I was able to keep piano tuning, and I didn't find that it was that big of an issue for me at all. I seemed to quickly adapt and carry on as usual and nobody knew anything except me and my immediate family. I did, however, find it much more difficult to play and sing and to do recordings and things of that nature because there was not a true balance of hearing between my two ears. I managed it and just moved forward and slowly allowed myself to adapt to the entire situation.

Things were not over yet with my ear issues either and as it turned out after quite some time; I started developing more of a muffled sound in my bad left ear again. This time the muffled sound in my bad ear was not from infection, so I went back to the ear surgeon once again for a hearing test and to have him take a look and see what was going on. As it turned out he said, "Will, you've developed some scar tissue over the skin grafted area and that was causing a slight thickening of the graft." He did a variety of minor ear surgeries over time in my ear in the office, by going in and scraping some of the scar tissue away. It was extremely unpleasant, and I can't even describe what it felt like; because I was awake and there was nothing, they could give me to kill the pain. I had extreme pain in that area while it was happening, and I just took the pain as long as I could until I was yelling that I needed a break! That scraping of my eardrum continued for quite some time and eventually my ear surgeon said, "I think you need to go back in for surgery again." He said that he needed to really get in there and clean up the scar tissue. It was supposed to be a quick procedure, maybe about a half hour or so. So once again I quickly scheduled surgery and went back in under the knife. Unbeknownst to me, because I was knocked out, the surgery turned into a major ordeal, that lasted four to five hours. Raelene and my mom and dad were very worried about why it was taking so long. The surgeon finally came out and explained to Raelene and my parents why it took so long. He said, my left ear had to be removed and flipped to the side so he could operate properly and then sewn back on! While in recovery I finally became coherent, and the surgeon had informed me and my family that he ran into some very serious difficulties. He said that he really had not seen scar tissue like mine before. Apparently, I was in the one percent of the population that had the ability to develop too much scar tissue and that's exactly what happened in my bad ear. The abnormal amount of scar tissue ended up becoming invasive and going very deep and getting tangled up in a lot of other parts of my inner ear. My surgeon told me that he thought he was able to get it properly cleaned up, but I would have to keep an eye on it over time. All in all, the surgery seemed to be a success. I occasionally had to go in for some periodic small scraping and removing some scar tissue. My hearing in the left ear unfortunately seemed to be even a little worse after all those surgeries, major and minor. I was bummed out about that, but I adapted once again and just moved on with my work in my career and everything else in life.

One day I was looking in the mirror closely at myself and then it hit me; oh wow, my left ear was lower than my right ear and it was obvious! When the surgeon sewed my ear back on, he did not sew it on even with the right ear! I was baffled and extremely annoyed to say the least. This was part of the reason I had more hearing loss too, because my ear was not in the right position, it was not catching the incoming sound exactly as it had been before, but I was stuck with it. That was something that if I were a surgeon, I would never ever get wrong. I am a perfectionist, and I would have made sure the patient's ear was sewn on straight! The surgeon knew that I was a piano tuner too, so I thought he would have been a lot more precise. I was extremely frustrated once again, but I adapted to it and continued to work really without any problems for some surprising reason. Yes of course, I missed the hearing that I used to have, especially when it came to playing and singing and things like that. Yet oddly enough as far as my work as a piano tuner was concerned, if anything, I felt like I became stronger and much better over time.

At one point I decided to try out a small hearing aid, but it never felt right with me. My clients didn't even question me because at the same time cell phone earpieces just hit the market, so they thought that was what I was wearing. One day,

I accidentally lost the hearing aid, and I panicked. I was two thousand dollars down the drain, and I did not have the money to replace it at that time. It was strange at first, but after a few days I adapted once again, particularly with my piano tuning ability. I suddenly realized that I was tuning better without the hearing aid, than with it. I had specific criterion when I worked, and I really noticed a difference. How could this be I thought? I was now going back to working with my true hearing loss from my injury and all the surgeries. However, my tunings were better and in fact, better than they had ever been in my career. At the same time, I also began to realize that after years in the piano tuning business, I was getting in an even more enlightened state overall. I was way more in tune with things around me than usual and especially when it came to my work. I was in a much higher state of consciousness in general.

I had decided to bring someone in to shoot a very short video clip of me working on some advertising that I needed to do. I was tuning an amazing ancient piano from 1878; I had never seen myself while I was working, but I was quite surprised when I watched the video clip back. It was very clear that I was off in another place and in a very deep meditative zone while I worked. You could see it in my facial expressions, that I was working in a deep subconscious state. I was not aware that I worked like that to that extent, until I saw it. The video also provided me with all the answers I needed as to why I could possibly tune better than I ever had in my career. Despite the initial injury, and surgeries that I had sustained, I overcame it in quite an amazing way. Then it all clicked in my mind and began to make sense. I had connected with not only piano tuning but many other things in my life and around me in an even deeper vibrational and spiritual way. I had always been connected vibrationally to a very deep level my entire life, but my career greatly enhanced it over time. Basically, I was in an extremely different state of mind and consciousness while I was working, unlike other piano tuners. I had really heightened myself to an extraordinary level. It remarkably allowed me to adapt to my injury while in that extremely highly sensitive vibrational state. I couldn't really say that there were not others like me in the industry, but I did feel that I was extremely unique, because of my situation and all the trauma that I went through. It was truly amazing that my traumatic left ear injury had forced me to tap into resources much deeper than I could have ever imagined.

I could finally understand that the body, mind and spirit was an amazing vehicle that we were all blessed to be given. It could absolutely adapt and adjust, if we just allowed ourselves to recognize those vibrational adaptations. It was quite possible that I would not have become that extraordinary caliber of piano technician if I was not so deeply connected on a subconscious vibrational level. That connection and recognition of my adaptations allowed me to overcome my severe injury, that would have surely ended most other piano technicians' careers.

12

DEEPER AWAKENING

After years of peaceful work and normal interactions with family and friends, another life shift was creeping in upon me. I would also soon be given life's greatest gifts while going deeper still into my vibrational world. I could not foresee the joys that awaited me or the advancement of my perception of all around me, but as usual, I embraced it all head-on with acceptance.

I was now finally somehow in my thirties, and my younger days seemed like just a blip in time. I spent many hours of many days and many years tuning pianos, in what was basically a meditative state while working. I didn't think much of it at all; for me, it was just natural and how I approached the job. Nonetheless, it was affecting me increasingly more, and it was also being pointed out by those around me. My wife Raelene would often say when I got home from work, "You need to come back down; you are not grounded." By that she meant I was still walking around in this slightly meditative state most of the time. Even when I came home from work, I would often miss certain little key things around me. I even missed conversations because my mind was off in another place. I eventually became very aware of it, and I understood why it had happened to me. I felt as though it was a great benefit with my piano tuning work. It allowed me to be in touch with the instruments on a different level than other piano technicians could ever have imagined. I was constantly reminded of my regression with Laura and the knowledge given to me by Ecne, the glowing one. Vibrations and frequencies were what I worked with every day for many hours. I began to feel that it was important for people to realize that every living thing around them—and even non-living things—had a very real vibrational component to them. It was undetectable to most people who were not aware or awakened. I also knew there were many levels of being awakened, and it was very different for every person who was part of the process. That sort of understanding or knowing—or feeling of the subconscious things around us—could also run in family members as well.

During those years in my thirties, Raelene and I were blessed with three beautiful and remarkable children. It was my belief that this was the greatest gift you could ever receive on your journey through life. Our firstborn was a beautiful baby girl named Keelin. Two years later, another beautiful baby girl named Kira joined the family. Finally, five years later, a wonderful baby boy named Casey arrived and rounded out the Campbell clan. I didn't need to look much further than my own children to see varying spiritual connections within them.

Keelin, my oldest, was very open from a soul level. She was also very emotional, so when she was happy, you knew it. When she was mad, you knew it as well because she really expressed it. She also had great spiritual awareness that came to her from me, Raelene, and her grandmother Polly. Unfortunately, Keelin did not always feel a good presence around her at times. She was the one that could get some creepy and scary stuff that would come around her. Nonetheless, she was very aware of things on a significant vibrational level.

My youngest daughter Kira was also highly spiritual and extremely connected with the Earth. That connection was also really evident with her even from a very young age. She would blurt out the most profound sayings when she was just a small child, that were coming from another place. She would talk about before her birth, when she could see before her eyes had opened. She also spoke of her older sister, saying, "Keelin was always my sister." As the years passed, she too had a very deep spiritual awakening. Kira was also an empath for many of our deceased relatives and others that would connect with her at various times.

Ah, and then there was my son Casey. He looked at the world in a logical and black-and-white sense. He loved nature and enjoyed the serenity of it. He was also very good with animals and people. Maybe the world needed balance from those who could see things from a more traditional, mainstream sense. I do have to say that he was the most stable emotionally and logically when there was stress around him. He was on his way, I suppose, to later connections to his deeper self. Those sorts of things only present themselves when and if the time was right for anyone along their own journey.

I did a lot of custom woodworking and building in our house. Each project was unique and different. One of my favorite pieces was a large, custom-built bookcase I made for my office, something you couldn't just buy in a store.

When my dad, Ed, came over and saw the bookcase, he was unusually quiet. But a few days later, I received a letter from him. That was how he expressed himself when it came to important things.

In the letter he went on and on about how proud he was of me. He said he was astounded by the bookcase and couldn't believe I had built it. He described the craftmanship as absolutely outstanding and said he was so proud that I had paid attention to all the things he had taught me.

What touched me the most was when he wrote that it was uniquely mine, something that not even he could have created.

That letter meant a tremendous amount to me. It was the confirmation I had hoped for from him, validation of my abilities and all the years I had put into learning and building. I was extremely grateful for his guidance all those years.

Well, my work continued to be so deeply meditative, and that state of mind carried with me throughout every day. Lots of feelings, vibes, intuition, whatever you wanted to call it, came to me all day. The flooding of those things just continued to intensify over time. Working in such a peaceful meditative state had also led to a lot of creativity within my head for various projects. The projects sometimes were ones that I was currently working on or planned to work on in the future. Often, I would even work on writing and composing music in my mind. Most of those things that I did were well thought out in my mind ahead of time. Later I would just put into action what I had already thought out beforehand. Of course, I also found it necessary to tweak and adjust some things as I got further involved in a particular project. For the most part, the blueprint was already laid out during my meditative states.

I believed it was also important for other people to listen to their inner voice, even if there were things that they didn't always want to hear. I truly believed that those deep vibrational messages were there to guide us through our life. That was the deep part of us that connected us to everything around us in the universe—it was the great universal vibrational connection. If you were someone who took that for granted or had no recognition whatsoever, I felt that it would be a shame for you to miss out on those experiences. The term "mind's eye" was there for a reason; all you had to do was allow it to open and allow yourself to see on a different level. Then you could finally begin to look at all the things around you differently. I wanted others to not miss the opportunities to see what most would never see. Unfortunately for me, even some dark, disturbing things slipped through and presented themselves. Some of those things would really challenge my mental strength, as I would have to learn to navigate some very troubling negative energies moving forward.

MORNING HORROR

Wow, so here I was, Will Campbell, now in my early forties, and somehow my thirties had just slipped away from me. Sometimes in life, we could experience events that were a mystery and left us baffled as to how or why they occurred. For me, one such event would unfold and leave me searching for answers for many years. Most of all, it would rock me to my core and leave a long-lasting imprint upon me and how I handled all that was coming through to me in my more awakened state of consciousness.

I was living in Warrington, Pennsylvania, and life was as normal as it could be for me to raise a young family. One day I retired from the evening as usual and fell into my typical sound sleep. I generally slept like a rock. When I woke up the next morning, my eyes slowly opened, and there was a slight glimpse of sunlight outside the window. It was a beautiful clear morning. I had a habit of opening my eyes slowly due to a previous incident. Once before, I opened my eyes too quickly and ripped the cells off the surface of my eyeballs, from my eyelids stuck to them. It was extremely painful, and I was careful not to allow it to happen again. I was alone in bed, and as I slowly awakened, the vibrational energy around me felt very dark and intense. I suddenly sat up in bed and proceeded to have a very clear, vivid vision. This vision was extremely disturbing and graphic. I was wide awake and by no means asleep whatsoever. I was shockingly seeing a murdered woman! I did not see how she was murdered or by whom, but all the other details were there right in front of me. I was frozen in terror as things unfolded. I could not believe what I was seeing! It was like I was sitting right there! She had shoulder-length dirty blond thick hair. Her eyes were wide-set, and she had very white skin. She was also wearing a light blue dress. I could also see an old-style army blanket near her. It was so hard to process and painful to see. Things started to get more fragmented, and then just pieces of information would come through. I was horrified, but I still wanted more details. I could tell that her body had been moved, either from the original murder scene or that she had been buried and then moved and buried in a different location near or in water. Things started to dissipate even more, and I was grasping for more information. I also felt so connected to it that I could feel all the emotions associated with the tragic scene. I could feel her emotions of fear and deep sadness, as well as a strong feeling of guilt and regret from whoever had taken her life. I felt that this was not premeditated but somehow snowballed into a tragedy that just got worse and out of hand. I could not see any more details and was getting frustrated, but at the same time, wished I had never seen it at all. After a while, it was all over. I was still sitting up in bed, stunned by what had unfolded. I did not move at all; I just tried to process all of it. I was still tied to all the emotions of it all as well. It was a lingering deep pain and sadness that I could not shake off. I could not understand why I saw this, and I was terrified. The horrific event started to create havoc in my mind greatly, and it made me begin to question myself as a person. I started to wonder if I really knew who I was! I had so much detail about that event that I began to wonder if it was somehow suppressed memories within me. How and why could I have so much detail? I had often experienced and seen many things since I was a young child, but nothing of that magnitude, and that was personally extremely disturbing to me. I began to take on more emotions of the person responsible for the murder, but I could not rationalize it at all. I even had the thought and wondered if it was me! I pondered if I was an evil person and all the sadness and hurt that it would bring to my family. None of it made any sense; it was just wrecking my mind. I tried to relax and go into a meditative state and get more information, but it was useless. I was truly emotionally hurt and scared by what had unfolded before me.

I eventually went downstairs and ate my breakfast and never said a word to anyone and tried to go about my day. However, inside of me, I could not shake it, and I pondered it repeatedly and tried to get more answers. I finally headed out to work that day and was working up in the Allentown area of Pennsylvania. I went into my first piano tuning call; it was a regular client of mine. I began to work on the piano, and then the woman of the house said to me, "Did you hear what happened?" I replied no, because I was not from the area, and she had just assumed that I might have known what she was referring to. She then proceeded to tell me that a young woman had been murdered nearby and that it was done by someone close to her in the neighborhood who may have had some mental issues. I turned to her and asked her if she was wearing a blue dress. She said she was not sure, because details like that would not be released to the public that early on. She seemed puzzled by my response, to say the least. I did not say anything else to her, and part of me was relieved because the coincidence was quite remarkable. Unfortunately, there were still too many unknown questions for me, and I could not let it go mentally at that point. The whole event lingered and festered for me for nearly three months and almost cost me my marriage from the stress I was in. I still had not told anyone, not even Raelene at the time. I kept trying to revisit it in my mind and retrieve more details to complete the picture, but nothing seemed to work. I even went as far as investigating unsolved murders within a certain time, by going by the hairstyle that I had seen on the victim. I even went back to my childhood home to see if there were any memories that would come back to me. Keep in mind that this event was so vivid that I was doubting the true nature of the vision and filling in the blanks with myself because I had no other explanation. No other information came forward to me no matter what I did or how I investigated it. I was deeply tortured by the whole disturbing vision. I eventually couldn't take it anymore and finally told my wife Raelene what was going on and why I had become so unraveled. She told me that I most likely had a lucid dream and that it was never truly real to begin with. I didn't believe that because I had seen many things since I was a child, but this was very different for me. Also, in this circumstance, I was sitting up wide awake in bed when it happened, and I was confident of that. Unfortunately, the horrific event never really went away for me.

I did at one point have my friend Laura over, who had stepped me through my past life regression—the one when I saw myself as an old man. At that point, she said that she had been working with police departments around the country for help with unsolved murders. I told her about the event and asked her if she could possibly help me with the disturbing vision I experienced. Instead, she asked me what I could foresee for her, since we were both wired the same. I think she had more faith in my abilities than her own; I was not sure. After my brief meeting with Laura, our lives drifted apart, and I never saw her or Ted again. This was yet again another dead end in my search for answers to what had happened. For me, it was just more frustration after a long period of time from the initial event. My mental torture would go on and on, and there were no clear answers for me to the tragic event. For the time being, I was forced to somehow try and escape all the trauma that I endured from that strange occurrence as best that I could.

Native Walking

One day Raelene and a close friend decided to bring in a guy from the Midwest area of the United States for a visit. He was a famous hypnotist and a past life regression specialist. They went ahead and set up a group meeting with some family and friends and him at our house for a group regression session. The guy's name was Gary. My initial instincts of him were not that impressive. Lots of people could learn to step you through regressions and do hypnotism. There were countless books written on those topics. A lot of it came down to how open people were and receptive to things like that, so of course I was going to be able to utilize the session.

This was different than my last past life regression because it was in a group setting. I paid no attention to the group at all. I just focused on myself and relaxed and let things come to me. Once again, I landed in a different place in time. Just as it was last time, I was fully aware of both realms, the living room I was in and the past at the same time. I suddenly found myself looking down at my feet and seeing moccasins. I thought to myself, wow, this is so cliché, I'm an Indian? I was almost amused by it, but it was very clear. I was a younger Indian boy named Achak, meaning spirit. I was with my father, whose name was Mohegan, meaning "person of the wolf." We were from the Algonquin Indian tribe, and they inhabited the Ottawa River Valley, which was part of what is now Quebec and Ontario, Canada. I could see that we were in the forest together, and my father was teaching me to hunt. He taught me to walk quietly, making no sound. He also taught me about the rippling spirit of the forest and how everything was connected. We were part of those connections, and therefore we needed to respect all things living in the forest along with the land that was provided to us by Mother Earth. That life that I was viewing was going by me very quickly, like a movie on fast forward. I also saw my wife named Aiyana, meaning eternal blossom. I cried when I saw her. I could hear her singing a water song about the flowing lifeblood of us and Mother Earth. I also saw myself with many tribal members and elders in a ceremony at the sacred rocks. I was shown the pictures on the giant rocks that had been put there by our great ancestors. The pictures told the story of the glowing ones who came from the sky and gave us fire and taught us the ways of Mother Earth and the great universe. I could also see that the great spirits had blessed me with many children and grandchildren. I eventually went through my own death in my old Algonquin life in that regression. My main thought as I was dying was, I hoped that I had done enough for those around me in that lifetime. I could feel myself thinking while I was dying, oh great spirit and Mother Earth, please tell me I did enough. Slowly, I could feel myself lifting out of that lifetime and venturing back to my living room. It was very emotional for me, from happiness to great sadness. In the end, it was another gift bestowed upon me. It made certain things yet again clearer to me—like when I would walk quietly along the creek like an Indian when I was a little boy with my dad, Ed. I finally understood how I was able to do that in my current lifetime. After everything was over, I began to reflect on the vision of the traumatic murder I had seen yet again. As Gary was leaving, I asked him if he had ever done any private regressions for something specific. He said yes, he had, and he was going to be in town for a few more days if I wanted to set something up. I said yes, I would like to do that. I then made an appointment to meet him at the hotel he was staying at. Keep in mind a lot of time had passed, but I was still grasping for answers from my previous horrific vision.

I finally met Gary at the hotel for my appointment, and I began to give him a brief description of what had happened to me. I told him that I wanted to do another regression to see if I could get any more information on the horrific event. I don't think he was expecting that sort of thing, but he was making money, so he was willing to do it. I sat in a chair in the hotel room, and he slowly walked me back into a hypnotic state through another regression. I could tell I was headed in the right direction because my body began to go into a rhythmic motion.

Specifically, my right arm was going back and forth like the second hand on a watch in front of me. That sort of thing was common in hypnotism and regression. I did finally connect with the murdered woman, but much of the same information was there and not any more specifics on the initial event. I remember her saying that she was OK, and that she was at peace and had moved on. I finally came out of the deep meditative regression, and I did feel a little sense of relief. Gary, on the other hand, seemed a bit uneasy with me, and I could tell that we just did not click. Keep in mind that Gary was somebody who had learned how to do past life regressions through the process of hypnosis. He was not necessarily someone who was like me, that had any experiences like me throughout his life. I felt as though he too could not comprehend it, and he did not understand me and may have even been a little frightened by the information. I was OK with that, and it really didn't matter what he thought, because I never had to see him again anyway.

After years of wondering and torment from my traumatic vision, I decided to just let it all go and be at peace with it. There was nothing more I could do. I could not go to the police because they would think I was crazy, and there was just not enough information to piece it all together. Maybe the lady in Allentown was right about the murder after all, and maybe I just picked up on the vibrational thread of that event. We are all connected vibrationally through good or bad events. That was definitely a very bad event for me, for sure. That disturbing set of circumstances was something that I truly wished that I had never experienced. A release from that tragic event and all the emotions tied to it were all that was left for me to do. So, I had to finally release that torturous vision, and forward was my only path in my current life.

13

HEALING AND DEATH

Well, my late forties just rolled up upon me before I knew it, and the Campbell clan was rolling right along as well. During those years I also learned a lot about life, but healing and death were the things that I felt on a much deeper vibrational level. I would have to learn how to navigate those flowing life forces and energies as best I could on my journey through life.

For as far back as we could trace our version of man and most likely into the future, birth and death was a constant certainty. The in-between part of our life itself was the only variable. Our lives really had countless flexibility. Even from a health standpoint, the variables were enormously vast. For eons mankind had questioned life, sickness, death, and healing. Humans had always struggled with death and why and when it came. Many religious organizations around the world taught that death was the will of their God, creator, or higher power. Then you had the skeptics and sometimes even those within those religions that would say, why did death have to come to a baby who was only minutes old? Why did a young child have to be taken by a tragic accident? Was it reasonable to think that a God or higher power was up there spinning the wheel of life and—oh my—some child's number just came up. Seriously, we needed to be more rational about it than that. Unfortunately, some things just happened in life, and acceptance was all that was left. From the moment that we were born, the forks in the road of life came to us every second of our existence. All of us were forging who we were and what we would become by the forks we chose. There would always be an enormous number of outside sources that altered us and our paths in life. Throughout our history, healers, shamans, and prophets or visionaries were prevalent. So many people had sought out one of the so-called healers to help them or a loved one. Was healing from a spiritual level possible? There have been countless accounts of individuals with healing powers, or as I like to refer to it, as people with a deeper vibrational connection. Why did some seem to have those exceptional gifts? And why did those incredible gifts not always work?

As I went through my later forties, I became more aware of the energy flowing in me, particularly from my left hand. I felt that I could feel and sometimes move or compress the energy around me or others at certain times. I used to play a little game with my kids called "Close your eyes and tell me when you can feel me touching your face." I could get them to feel the energy from my hand on their face from three feet away. I also really felt drawn to family members, mostly who were in critical situations in the hospital. I was compelled to spend time alone with those family members to transfer energy to them and to help them in crisis situations. I felt that I had helped loved ones at times and then nothing in other situations. I by no means considered myself a miraculous healer. I just believed that sometimes I could channel positive energy to those who were in a weakened state. This did not mean that people like me could miraculously fix every ailment coming down the pike. I also did not fully understand everything I was feeling and why I felt it.

In a quest to get more answers, I decided to enroll in a local Reiki healing class. Everyone else in the class was pretty much there due to their own illness or someone else close to them. I was different; I wanted to validate what I was feeling, and I hoped to gain more knowledge too. I questioned the Reiki master named Melonie on what I was feeling, including being left-hand dominant with those energies. I felt that she knew I was different than the others in the class. I eventually became certified in Reiki levels one and two. At the end of my Reiki Level Two class, we were asked to pick one gemstone from a box that we felt drawn to. I picked a gem connected to intuition, which was no surprise to me. We also did an exercise in a group where we selected a name from the group out of a hat. We had to talk about what we felt about that person. I selected the person sitting to my left and described in detail about their male family member in the military. I was very much correct, and that was not my thing—I just went with my instincts. I didn't pursue things any further to become a Reiki master. I felt that I received all I needed from the classes, and I realized that for some reason, I was more drawn to those close to passing instead of healing. I did not even consider making money off Reiki healing; I did not feel that was the proper direction for me..

The wonderful teachings from my Reiki master Melonie helped me greatly in understanding a lot of the energy flow that

I was in tune with. It validated my own perceptions of that energy and how to channel it better when I needed it. Melonie had reached out to me many times about becoming a Reiki Master, as well as auditing some of the lower-level classes, but I knew it wasn't my true path. Melonie and I parted ways, but I took those important life lessons with me on my journey forward.

HEALING

I was still very attracted to that inner sense of healing energy that flowed through me. I just could not ignore it even though I knew that my possible deeper calling was to those closer to passing on. My feelings on both lingered on in my subconscious self and I was always aware that I may need to sometimes tap into those vibrational forces within me.

At one point, Raelene's father Mac went to the hospital for a heart valve replacement. While Mac was in recovery he developed very some serious complications. Things did not look good for him at all. All I could focus on was finding a bit of alone time with him. Eventually I found an opportunity and I proceeded to quietly sit beside Mac. I felt the intense vibrational energy building up in my left hand. I placed my hand above his chest, and I just focused a positive energy flow through me to him. My hand was very hot as we connected. Mac was not awake during that event. After a while I quietly left his bedside. Not long after he began to slowly gain strength. I never said anything to anyone, but Mac's wife Polly seemed to take notice of what had happened. I felt that the universal energy helped him, not me. I was just a conduit for that positive energy flow.

OUR SECRET RHYTHM

A few years later there was another event involving Raelene's mother Polly that challenged me greatly from a healing standpoint. There were very few people in my lifetime, that had such a profound effect on me from the moment I met them like Polly did. For me, I always called her mom out of respect. When I first met Polly, her husband Mac thought that his daughter had brought home the meat head. You know, the long-haired, flip flop wearing a kind of dude. Over time, me and him would get past that and we developed a good relationship. Polly, however, accepted me from the beginning. We had a strong connection immediately and it grew even stronger over time. I had an immense amount of respect for her, and to me she had a great understanding of life. Polly completely understood people and never judged them under any circumstance. She was an extremely spiritual woman, with some magnificent spiritual abilities of her own. Polly had a very high and in tune spirit with the universe. Sometimes she would see auras around people and even bad shadowy figures. We had many great discussions together on all sorts of spiritual topics but never any deep discussions on healing. We connected spiritually and I was truly blessed to have her in my life. Polly was born in Arizona, in a magnificently beautiful area, and she was very much connected with the land there, as was I after I went there. Often me and Polly would take off on little mini vacations together, down to the New Jersey shore and other things too. I always felt completely comfortable around her, and I loved her very much.

Unfortunately, Polly was diagnosed with COPD lung disease in her early fifties, and it was incredibly difficult for her and the family. At that time, there were no medications to prolong things for people diagnosed with that disease, so she suffered quite a bit. Polly had to drag an oxygen tank around with her and her disease just got progressively worse. She eventually went on a lung transplant list and finally one day, that dreaded call came in, and it was her time to go. So, she went and had the difficult lung transplant operation performed on her. In the beginning, things seemed okay, but it was an extremely difficult procedure to have done on anyone. The outcome at that time was only fifty percent success rate at best. Things started to really go downhill for her quickly, and she was having some difficulty with the aftereffects of the operation.

I was out working one day when Raelene called me and said, "My mom wants you to come to the hospital, only you." So, I left immediately to head to downtown Philadelphia, at the University of Pennsylvania Medical Center, per her request. I remember driving down route I-95 thinking why did she only want me to come down with all the other family around her. I thought, well maybe she wants to get her affairs in order, should something bad happen. Maybe Polly just felt a sense of comfort talking to me. Then something went off in my head, and I thought to myself, that's not it, she knows! By that, I meant that she knew that I sometimes tried to give healing energy to people around me in critical situations. Even though we had never discussed that, I was sure she knew it. When I arrived at the hospital, I walked into the room where Polly was and she tilted her head towards me and smiled and said, "I'm glad you're here, I want you to do what you do." Those words had confirmed what I had already thought that she needed some healing from another realm. That vibrational healing energy was going to come through me, as best as it could be. She closed her eyes as I placed my hands over her chest and lungs, where the surgeons had performed the operation. I did not touch her but merely kept my hands above her body while meditating and let the healing energy flow through me to her. After I was done, Polly thanked me, and I hugged her, and I told her that I loved her.

We both hoped all would be a little better moving forward. I felt that I did what came natural to me. I was shy about it and for the most part, I didn't like to discuss it. I didn't want to be looked at as a crazy person. Truthfully most people didn't understand the true concept of vibrational energy transfer. Sometimes I did think the process helped some people in the short term, and others may be longer. It could be mentally quite a burden, because I wanted to help with everything in my soul. I also had to be a realist and understand that some things could not be fixed. Unfortunately, some outcomes were inevitable and just part of the universal circle of life.

Polly made it out of the hospital and came back home in time for the Christmas season. She had quite a burst of energy and a beautiful glow about her as she prepared for the holidays. She got all her gifts for the family, and she was always so proud to be a part of her family. She was truly the matriarch on that side of the family, and she was very profound in her role. Things unfortunately quickly took a turn for the worse and Polly wound up back in the hospital. There apparently were some complications with the lung transplant and things just weren't going well at all. She had some follow-up work and monitoring of the lung transplant. The medical staff seemed to have stabilized her and got her back on track with her recovery.

One morning, Raelene and I headed to a popular local restaurant to have breakfast. On the way we called Polly while she was still in the hospital, and she sounded pretty good over the phone. So, for us there were no worries and things seemed to be progressing well with her. We went into the diner and sat down at a table in the back and had a brief conversation. Suddenly out of the corner of my left eye, I watched the coffee pot that the waitress had set on the table, slowly spin in front of me. I thought I was seeing things, so I briefly put it out of my mind, but I also wanted to be sure of what I saw. I continued our conversation and once again the coffee pot spun around all by itself! At that point, I jumped up and made a big scene about the place having a ghost or something of the sort. It was quite unusual, but we still didn't think that much of it and dismissed it. About ten minutes later while driving back home from our breakfast, we got a call from another family member regarding Polly. The hospital had contacted her first for some reason, instead of us and she was hemming and hauling about what was really going on. I told her to just give it to us straight! With that she said,

"There had been an emergency and Polly passed away suddenly!"

Raelene began screaming in utter horror of those words and she was completely inconsolable. I too was stunned and extremely upset. Apparently where the incision had been made to reconnect the new lung, there was a rupture, and she basically bled to death quickly. The truth was that her tissues had weakened from all the steroids she had been on overtime, and it prohibited the healing process in that area. The lung transplant never really had a chance of ever healing properly. A great magnificent woman was taken from us and the earth suddenly. Losing Polly, crushed me with extremely deep sadness. The family of course was devastated, and my children were at a tremendous loss at a young age. She was the perfect grandmother to them, and we could never replace her. We were forced to go through the funeral ceremonies and the burial as anyone would be, but it was particularly devastating right before the Christmas holidays. A great friend of Polly's sent a friend of the family to deliver all the Christmas presents that Polly had prepared for us. Many friends and family members stepped up for us and we were immensely appreciative. Sadly, this was a loss we could not overcome and for me, one that I would never fully recover from. I deeply missed her and knew I would for the rest of my life.

Much of the dynamic within the family was lost when Polly passed away. She would've kept a lot of things in check and believe me we all needed her guidance. I was tormented by not being able to possibly give her a little bit more of myself through vibrational healing energy. I tried many times to connect with her in deep meditation after she passed, but she would never come through. The funny thing is, often, the ones you want to come forward do not at all, they're usually the ones you don't expect. Very few people that you meet are a once in a lifetime great spiritual being. Polly would always be that beautiful soul for me. I missed Polly, I deeply loved Polly, and I hoped that she would always watch over us from above when we needed her. I was eternally thankful for Polly being such an incredible part of all our lives.

DEATH

Death was an inescapable part of not only our own existence but also those around us. I understood that accepting the passing of a loved one was a process we must all face. You could look at our bodies as merely a biological machine with a shelf life. The machine was driven by our soul or life force. I knew that our soul was vibrationally connected to everything. Death was merely a multilayered process and could vary depending on the circumstances. Vince, my time traveler friend, had reinforced that knowledge to me. Many people truly feared death, but what they really feared was the unknown. Even those who professed to have strong religious beliefs feared death; they just wouldn't admit it. Did we really want to live to crazy ages?

We were all obsolete before we even realized it. If you thought about it, by the time we even hit our eighties, we all longed for life in our younger days, no matter how much we tried to convince ourselves otherwise. I knew that we must move on through the process and accept our soul's transformation. Sometimes we needed a little nudge to accept our death and let go. My dad Ed's death was a perfect example of that.

My dad always told me that he did not want to linger on if he was in a critical situation. One day he went in for emergency cancer surgery that was a success, but due to years of smoking, he could not regain normal breathing after the surgery. He suffered for an extended period and eventually went on a ventilator, something he never wanted. Unfortunately, even though I knew this, he did not have a living will to state his true wishes. My mom Mary was calling the shots and did not have the strength or understanding to let him go. They were married for sixty-three years and together even longer. It was a tremendous pressure on my mom, I understood that, but I was angry too. I controlled as much as I could from behind the scenes. I, of course, attempted some Reiki healing on him many times, but some things were inevitable, as hard as that was to accept. Finally, the day of passing would come for my dad. I called all the close relatives to come to the hospital to say their goodbyes. He had coded several times the night before, and they just kept bringing him back. For some reason, the family all went to the cafeteria except for me and my mom. I finally had enough, and so did my dad, but I knew he was hanging on for my mom. She was always very dependent on him their whole lives. They were a beautiful team and enjoyed a long life together; it was a complete love story. My dad was unconscious for an extended period at that point, so me and my mom just sat at his bedside. I spoke to my father in my mind and told him that I loved him and thanked him for all that he had taught me about life. I then told him it was OK to let go and be at peace; I would make sure that I took care of my mom for him. And with that subconscious communication between him and I, my dad let go immediately. The heart monitor in front of me began to drop rapidly, and I leaned over to my mom and told her that we had to go, because the doctors and staff were going to come in. I knew as they all rushed in while we were leaving the room, that he would not come back this time. After he passed, I came back in and put my hands on his arms to see and feel the tattoos he had, just as I did when I was a small child, one last time.

With that, my hero, my mentor, and the greatest person that I ever met was gone.

Before my mom, Mary, reentered the room, she did one of the most incredible things I had ever seen. In her darkest, most painful moment of her life, after losing her greatest love, her best friend, and soulmate, she somehow found the strength to do something truly remarkable.

She approached the doctor who had tried to save my dad. He looked slightly startled as she walked toward him. Honestly, I think he was bracing for some kind of confrontation, expecting anger or blame because he hadn't been able to save my dad.

But instead, she lifted her head, looked him in the eye, and thanked him, genuinely for all he had done. Then she wished him peace and love in his own life.

It was extraordinary. Through overwhelming grief, she was able to set her own pain aside, even for a moment, to offer kindness and grace. I could never forget it.

My oldest daughter, Keelin, was the only one who didn't know that my dad had passed away because she was away on a trip in the mountains. We decided to wait to tell her so she wouldn't be upset while driving back.

When she returned home, I took her into my office and gently told her that her Pop Pop Ed had passed away. Keelin was devastated by the tragic news. She was his first grandchild and very close to him. He had even taught her the word *apple*, her first word-other than "mom" and "dad".

I didn't want to leave her, but I was completely exhausted, both physically and mentally, so I told the family I needed to go upstairs and rest. Shortly after, I was awakened by loud screaming and yelling downstairs. When I came down to see what was going on, Keelin said she saw Pop Pop looking in the window, and I believed her, because she was always sensitive to things like that.

The rest of the family was also a bit shaken because they noticed green glowing orbs flying around the kitchen. I asked everyone to go into another room and settle down. Then I sat quietly in the sunroom, which gave me a perfect view of the kitchen. I watched approximately six to nine glowing orbs, about the size of golf balls and draining in color, fluttered in a group around the soffit. I knew it was my dad. And honestly, it was comforting to see.

Keelin came back in and said, " Pop Pop, I'm happy you are here, but I don't want to see you." She was scared-so he faded away.

I knew he had come for her, because she would have been so distraught over his passing. My dad lingered for some time after his death, causing small disturbances with the cable boxes and other electronic devices, like the lights. We all knew it was him, and we'd say hello. Eventually he moved on.

Tragically, I found a note directing his medical wishes after his death. He left it for me along with countless letters to me as well as his family history. He also left letters to my children and Raelene about how proud he was of them, and how he viewed their individual spirits, and what he saw for them in the future. All his teachings of life and nature were hidden where only I would find them; he knew me all too well. I put them all together in a binder with a picture of a wolf on the cover—we called it Ed's Bible. He was the spirit of the wolf, just like my Algonquin Indian father Mohegan. The book was there for us to always reflect upon and draw wisdom from. What an amazing, precious gift he left all of us. I struggled with his loss for a very long time, and in some ways, it affected the course of my life. There was a massive void in my life, and it would take me years to really understand all that he taught me about life and death and the acceptance of it. His teachings of nature and the skills of great woodworking were priceless to me. There would never be a greater influence on my life than my dad Ed.

I understood that healing and spiritual energy flowed within all of us. It could be used as a tool to strengthen us and others at times, but some things were not meant to overcome. Death was just as much a part of us as was our life. It was all just as the Indians had taught me in my previous life. Our spirits were all vibrationally connected in the beautiful circle of Mother Earth and the great universe.

CHOICE OF NO RETURN

Over the years I had lost many friends and family who passed away but there were a few that passed away because they had unfortunately taken their own lives. The old saying that you had to walk a mile in someone else's shoes to truly understand them, was true. I could see that everyone had a breaking point and could be driven to those dark thoughts or even possibly self-harm. Under great stress anyone could feel that they might be better off dying, maybe it would be easier on everyone else! Truthfully, it was never easier on anyone else. It was painful, heart-wrenching and crippling to family and friends after someone had passed away from suicide.

The Campbell clan eventually moved into a brand-new development in Warrington Pa. It was a great area, with lots of young families. One of the families had two young children around the same age as my girls, and we met their parents. My children's new friend's mom was a tall, beautiful woman named Mia. She also looked forward to raising her children in the development and seemed full of life. She and other neighbors would gather out in front of our house to meet and greet each other and to share some excitement over the new development. Mia and I hit it off quickly, because we had shared a common past. Neither one of us was raised by our real parents, so we were able to share some experiences that were different from most people. There was some attraction between the two of us and some flirting from time to time but that was the extent of it. Overtime Mia would confide in me, regarding her past with her mother and some other childhood issues. She also confided in Raelene on things going on in her marriage as well.

While on a family vacation, we took a cruise to the Bahamas. We also had some friends on the ship; a couple from Boston named John and Julie. It was a typical cruise, a lot of food, sunshine and beautiful stops along the way. We were in our final night on the cruise and headed back from the Bahamas to New Jersey. We had planned to meet our friends for dinner and drinks that last evening. As we were about to head out to dinner, my kids were alerted suddenly through social media of an alarming circumstance that had unfolded. My kids informed Raelene and I that they were not sure if it was a misunderstanding, but the people were saying that Mia had passed away! None of us believed it at first but then after some further confirmation through social media, it unfortunately was confirmed. It got even worse from there, when we had learned that she had taken her own life! It was extremely shocking because not only was I close to Mia, but Raelene was a close confidant for her in times of stress. It was very overwhelming for all of us, including my children, who had spent years growing up as close friends of their family. Mia always welcomed our kids into her home like a second mom. Raelene was extremely distraught, because she felt that if she had been there, she may have been able to help Mia. Regretfully our beautiful friend had a lot of traumas in her life. Mia's mother and her best friend had both passed. She was also going through a divorce and a new relationship that was not a healthy one either. She was backed into a corner, and I suppose she felt that death was the only way out. I told our friends on the ship the news, and we would unfortunately not be able to spend the evening with them. The whole situation tortured me as I wandered around the ship, and I eventually headed back to the cabin. It was extremely emotional for everyone; Mia was way too young to pass away so tragically and leave her family to deal with a mess like that! I could not help but focus on her very intensely, and I was desperate for answers as to how she got to that final awful decision.

We finally retired for the evening and while in bed, Raelene and my young son were to the right of me. I decided to go into a very deep meditation, with hopes to possibly connect with

Mia. I was grasping for some sort of answers why she chose that horrible ending. I didn't know how a deliberate meditative reaching out to her was going to go. Sometimes something totally different could come through, that you were not expecting. Maybe it was the relaxing movement of the ship or the sound of the waves, but I was able to go into a very deep meditative state. My goal was to connect with Mia and speak with her through my mind and suddenly there she was! She came through to me and it was very clear and very emotional for me. I greeted her in my mind, and I attempted to get some answers regarding the tragedy. This was not like a normal verbal conversation. It came through in one big block of information all at once. It was like opening a small report and understanding everything in it within an instant. Mia had conveyed to me that she too was deeply saddened by the event. She did not really grasp the finality of it, even though it was premeditated. She had become a frequent drinker and just like drugs, that could push you over the edge in times of great stress. Mia took her life by asphyxiation in her car, in a garage in her new town home. She said that she was overwhelmed with grief, depression and the alcohol had made things much worse leading up to the end. Mia told me that if she had to do it over again, she would not have made that horrific choice. I felt as though the traumatic event was two folded; she was somewhat at peace and then also tormented by her irrational decision. While this was all going on, my body started to go into convulsions. Many times, while in a deep state of meditation or a past life regression, sometimes parts of the body could go into a vibrational rhythmic motion. It was usually within the arms or legs, with a steady back and forth movement of some sort. This was due to a deep connection on a vibrational level subconsciously, that eventually affected the physical body. However, for me this time it was my entire body, not just my arms and legs. So, I was totally convulsing in bed while the meditation was going on, and I was fully aware of it. I stayed locked in the moment with Mia, while also being aware of myself convulsing and worrying that I was going to wake Raelene or my son. In fact, I could not believe that they did not wake up right away, because of how violent the convulsions were. Eventually Raelene did wake up, and she thought I was having a heart attack in bed. While staying in tune with Mia, I was also able to tell Raelene that I was okay. I told Raelene that it was a vibrational thing, and I was now connected with Mia. I told Raelene not to worry about me, and I needed to speak to her much more. I was getting too distracted by having to deal with my physical side and keep assuring Raelene that I was okay. Eventually things had to dissipate between me and Mia, and I couldn't hang onto both realms any longer. I was very disappointed that I could not go further with my connection with Mia. I came out of the deep meditation extremely dehydrated. I kept getting up out of bed and just inhaling as much water as I could get. Eventually I calmed down and I just accepted the fact that at least I had made a connection, and I was very happy about that. I tried several times later to reconnect with Mia, but it never happened again.

Once back home, we had to deal with seeing the family and the tragic emotion of it all. I knew it was going to be different than some other funerals and even some other suicides that I had known about. Finally, the day of the funeral had arrived. It was understandably very emotional for everyone involved. My oldest daughter Keelin was sitting to the left of me, and I couldn't help but notice something very evident going on during the ceremony. Mia's children got up to speak and pay tribute to their deceased mother. Her son, the youngest of the two children, played some music on his guitar in tribute to his mother. Then Mia's daughter, the older child, gave a heart-wrenching speech addressed to her mother. It referred to the future for herself, of how life would be without her mother being there. While this was going on, I noticed an extremely bright and thick white aura around both her children and only them, not the preacher or anyone else there. It was obvious to me that was Mia there with them. I had been able to see auras for quite some time, but it was not something that I could see all the time. Usually, I had to be looking for it, and it was something that I believed you could learn to see if you were open minded enough. For me the best way to see an aura on a person was to look beyond the person while looking at them. It also helped to have some sort of neutral background but that was not always required. I was amazed by the aura around Mia's children. I leaned over to my daughter Keelin who was extremely distraught and crying heavily and said, do you see that? I did not say what I was seeing. She looked up and said to me, "yes I see that there is a glow or an aura around Mia's two children." Keelin had never seen that before in her life, but it was confirmed since both of us could see it. After the funeral I discussed it further with Keelin and explained to her what it was and how to see it around people. I already knew she was very open to a lot of things around her in general. Over the next few days Keelin became infatuated with the idea and looked for auras on everyone. She was pretty good at it, and she could see more than me in general. Keelin was able to see vivid colors in the auras of people. Like any teenager, she quickly googled the meaning behind the colors. She was so fascinated by what would show up around the people that she was looking at. I was very torn over the whole experience that I had on the ship and at the funeral as well. I was not sure if I should have said anything to Mia's family about connecting with her on the ship. I was not real close with her husband, and I just decided not to say anything; because I didn't know if they would believe me or not. I did not want to offend them, so I just let it go. I often wondered if I had made the right decision. In the end, Mia was a beautiful woman with a beautiful spirit. She just got lost in the stresses of life and made a horrible decision. Sadly, her family and friends would carry lasting scars from her terrible decision for the rest of their lives. I understood that you could never judge or criticize people going through depression and thoughts of suicide. They just needed more love and compassion. Sadly, all we could do was live and learn as we journeyed forward through life.

As a family we never fully recovered from the two great losses of Polly and Ed. We were all a bit mentally scattered.

Unfortunately, I also lost my foster mom Mary and my foster sister Liz as well. My mom Mary had beaten breast cancer once but sadly it returned and destroyed her body. Mary never got over losing my dad Ed and she finally succumbed to cancer. I was the only one with her when she passed. The staff at the hospice center asked me if I was one of them. Most of the volunteers there felt a call to assist people in their time of passing. They recognized that in me as well. Mary passed in her sleep right next to me, but I had fallen asleep. I was upset that I was not awake, but I felt that was how she wanted it. Another beautiful soul was taken from me and the family. Not too long after Mary's passing, I also lost my sister Liz from a very quick nasty battle with pancreatic cancer. She had survived a heart attack and open-heart surgery, but the aggressive cancer was swift and devastating to her. Unfortunately, all the death wasn't done with just them. I also lost a best friend and three of my real siblings. I lost my two brothers and oldest sister who were all products of traumatic child abuse which led to addiction and eventually their own deaths. I did, however, keep an open relationship with my two remaining birth sisters, Maggie and

Julie. For the most part my relationship with Julie was much closer, I think because we were closest in age. I suppose I even suffered from some survivor's guilt over all that loss. With having to bury that many people, I guess a part of me died with all of them. I also began to bury a lot of emotion along with it too. I could remember even being at one of the funerals and feeling like people were staring at me because I wasn't acting upset enough, but truthfully, I just didn't have anything left in the tank to give. Even though I understood death, I did not handle it well, because of its magnitude.

By the end of my forties that old midlife crisis fell upon us like another dark plague. Like a disastrous storm the relationship began to fracture between Raelene and me. It was like a train going a thousand miles an hour and running off the tracks. Sadly, Polly and Ed, the two people who may have kept the family balanced were gone. Raelene and I eventually divorced and amicably went our separate ways. Raelene eventually remarried to a wonderful man named Sam. Raelene and I remained friends, but the stress upon the whole family was unfortunately very difficult and everlasting for all of us.

14

RETURNING TO SKARA BRAE

Well, now that I, Mr. Will Campbell was entering my fifties; many life adjustments were inevitable. From business to love and deeper spirituality, new paths would unfold for me. Some of my dark past would always follow me, but a deeper and even stronger vibrational connection to the universe beckoned me to continue forward on my life's journey.

It was very difficult for me and my family after my divorce in many ways. The adjustment of a totally different family dynamic to the reorganization of my business was a tremendous struggle. While I was trying to find my way, I also occasionally attempted dating. For the most part, my dating endeavors were generally a waste of my time. I met too many damaged women and, quite frankly, I suppose I was damaged myself. I realized that I was in a selfish stage of my life and perhaps I should not have been dating at all. One day out of nowhere, I received a message from a woman. The message said, "Hi, I'm Gwen. I like your pics and profile. I think we have a lot in common, and I'd like to see where it goes." I messaged Gwen back, and we set up a date to meet. On our date, I was greeted by a very beautiful blonde-haired woman. Our conversation was as if we had known each other for hundreds of years, it was easy. Well, the truth is, we never separated from that night on and eventually got married. Gwen was very much like me and was also very deep. She told me later in our marriage that we were connected long ago and that she was me in her past life. I know it would probably sound crazy to a lot of people, but I understood it. We even had some friends comment on how we not only looked similar, but our mannerisms were very similar as well. Gwen was highly intuitive and spiritual, and she was very much connected to the earth. I felt that she was a very awakened spirit. Gwen had suffered since her teenage years with some serious illnesses. I truly believed that her fight throughout the years had grounded her and made her much more connected to people. Gwen had a tremendous understanding of life and the true things that really mattered. She suffered so much and had been on the brink of death many times. Even if her path was not the easiest one, she had an inner strength like no one I had ever known. We embraced our natural fit together and eventually bought a lovely house and enjoyed the times we had together with family and friends.

By my mid-fifties, my piano work was deeply subconscious, and I had been tuning pianos for thirty years. On my fifty-eighth birthday, my wife Gwen gave me a unique ring. The stone in it was called Moldavite. Gwen was a seasoned gemologist and really knew her gemstones well. I had asked her for that ring because of the uniqueness of the stone's properties. Moldavite was an amazing gemstone that came from meteors that hit the earth and transformed into a form of glass from roughly around fifteen million years ago. Its vibrational properties were extremely intense, especially for those who were sensitive to it. It could heighten our vibrational connection with the universe and assist in overall clarity of our being. The difference for me was almost immediately. Within about ten minutes of putting the ring on, I quickly started to feel high from the ring's vibrational energy. My piano tuning work was heightened to a point where I was doing even better tunings than I ever had in my life. I did not get the ring for that specific reason, but the effects on me were undeniable. Unfortunately, I lost the ring during the winter when I was removing my glove while I was walking my dog. I looked for it a lot, but I never found that amazing ring. I kept looking for another piece of Moldavite that would affect my vibrational energy the same way. I finally decided that I would find the right piece of Moldavite when the moment was right for me.

I had a wonderful client named Clara, who had worked with many people dealing with trauma through past life regressions. I had known Clara for many years, and we had always connected and had a lot in common. With all of Gwen's medical conditions over the years, there was a part of me that felt that she, just like me, may have had something in a previous life that may have been carried forward and affecting her current life. She had enough trauma from her younger years, and perhaps there was some connection to a past life that was unresolved. I thought that it might be beneficial for Gwen to maybe try to look to her deep past for answers regarding her health issues.

While I was doing some piano tuning work for Clara, I talked to her about Gwen and everything she had dealt with over the years. I talked to her about my suspicions about the possibility of her past lives affecting her life now. I asked Clara if she might be able to help Gwen to do a past life regression and see if there were any connections to her current life issues. Clara offered her services for free to take her through a past life regression and possibly reveal something that might provide some clues as to why Gwen had to struggle so much in this life. Clara also said to me that if I personally ever wanted to come in and work with her, her door was always open to me if the timing was right for both of us. For years, I never felt compelled enough to go to Clara personally for any spiritual work.

Gwen came in for the regression session with Clara for several hours one day. Gwen had told me about her regression and that it started off where she was a man, and she was in the crow's nest of a whaling ship. She said that her job was to spot the whales, but she refused to signal down to let the crew know that there were whales ahead because she did not want them to die. There was a lot more detail to that past life regression with Gwen, and it was fascinating for Clara as well, so they decided to do another session at our house another time. On the second session, Gwen's deceased father attempted to jump into her body, and Clara had stopped it just to be safe. Then when they resumed the regression, Gwen had found herself being beckoned by a group of aliens to come with them, and once again, Clara had stopped things out of concern for Gwen. Clara then stopped the regression altogether and later talked to other people in her line of work around the country about it. She felt that it was such an unusual event with the aliens, and she was looking for other opinions on that unusual regression. There was nothing definite that presented itself during Gwen's past life regression regarding her health issues.

Shortly after Gwen's regression, I started to feel compelled to reach out to Clara myself. I really didn't have a particular reason. Something inside me was just saying that this was the time for me to approach her after all those years. I called Clara and spoke to her about my interest in doing another past life regression with her, so we set up a session. She basically set a whole day aside for me altogether for the regression. I spent quite a bit of time in the beginning giving her a very detailed history of my life and who I was and where I came from. After I was done, she thanked me for sharing the information and started the process to step me through the past life regression. I was in a very comfortable reclining chair laying back. Clara asked me to continue to just take deep breaths and relax. She then told me to picture some clouds drifting by and to find one and just allow my spirit to drift slowly off with the cloud of my choice. I drifted high above the landscape on the cloud, and I totally let myself go and ease into this past life regression. Clara would periodically ask me what I saw, and I would describe the landscape in detail below me. Then I said I could see a village below me, so she asked me to head towards the village. I entered the village and found myself back in ancient times. The landscape was very green, the skies were slightly gray, and there was a beautiful river nearby. I could see a series of dwellings up in front of me. They were all ancient style round stone dwellings with a type of earth and thatched roof. The buildings were all round with a door and small openings for windows. Clara then asked me, "What do you see now?" I said that I saw people moving around the village, but it didn't seem as though they could see me. I felt like I was completely there in that village— mind, body, and spirit—and I was compelled to approach one smaller round dwelling. As I entered the door of that dwelling, I could see that there was a small stone table and a woman sitting at the table wearing a type of ancient Celtic garb. My initial feelings for her were that she was somebody very important in the village, so I slowly approached her. She slowly raised her head and looked at me and said, "I have summoned you, Paden." She said, "Your name means to be royal, and so shall you eternally be royalty." Somehow, I knew exactly who she was, and at the village, we all referred to her as Ban Leighis, "The Healer." She then told me that the glowing goddess of healing named Brigid came to her to ensure my destiny. She said to me, "Paden, your new journey awaits you as the new leader of Skara Brae. Most importantly, you will carry with you the knowledge of healing, strength, and enlightenment with the passing of your father Brennus." Ban Leighis was a great visionary, and she had a great connection to the spiritual world. She also told me that the transition of power was through fire and fire allowed the passing of the torch. She said that I must go to the body of my father Brennus to light the burial fire. I was deeply saddened and initially felt reluctant to light the fire under my father's body. Clara asked me again, "What do you see?" I told her that I was with all the people in the village preparing to light the fire for my father Brennus's burial. I did finally light the fire, and with that, all the emotion that goes along with the passing of a loved one went through me like a bolt of lightning. At the same time, I could also see all the villagers looking up to me, as this was a new beginning for me as the leader of Skara Brae. Clara then asked me to move forward in that lifetime, and I told her that I had also seen my wife Eilidh, meaning "torch" or "shining one." I also saw all my children and grandchildren there. Eventually, I found myself on my own deathbed in that life. I was very old, but I lived an honorable life. Once again, just like my regression with the Algonquin Indians, my thoughts as I was passing were: did I do enough for all those who needed me in my life? As I was passing from that lifetime, I could feel a tremendous vibrational energy surround me. Then I saw the glowing goddess Brigid, who gently smiled at me and told me to have no fear and move forward. I then began to hear Clara's voice quietly asking me to drift back on the cloud up and out of my regression to my current life.

That past life regression was another fascinating one for me, giving me a remarkable glimpse of my ancient roots in that Celtic tribe. It also gave me a better understanding of why I felt a lot of things in my current life regarding healing, confidence, and even death. After going through multiple regressions in my life, I understood that each time that I went back or forward in time, it was a unique and important passing of information to me. I occasionally stayed in touch with Clara over the years. Clara was truly another blessing in my life and someone that was very much wired like me. I was very grateful for her guidance through my remarkable, special journey back to Skara Brae.

15

THE LECTURES

I was now headed from my late fifties into my sixties. Moving into my forties and fifties did not really bother me, but to say I was in my sixties was rather odd. I thought, wow, Will Campbell, there was no denying that I was officially old and for sure in the fourth quarter of my life. The vibrational flow and connection to the Earth was greater than ever for me during my work and that period of life. I could sense more profound changes coming my way like a calm stream of rippling vibrational energy flowing towards me. At sixty years old, I was blessed with my first grandchild. My oldest daughter Keelin, now married to a creative man named Kevin, gave us all the greatest blessing of a beautiful baby boy named Quinn Harrison Sullivan. What a fine young lad he was. My heart was full of so much joy, to see his world unfold before him. Just like his Pop Pop, he was in love with drums. Any form of drumming would light up his soul, and you could see his connection to that ancient vibrational energy. I felt so blessed to have him in my life.

I decided that it was time for me to go to a more part-time schedule with my piano tuning work. I switched things to a three-day work week, allowing myself to have off every Friday through Monday. I viewed the change as a partial retirement for myself. It was nice, but I was still working nearly forty hours on the three days that I worked. One day, I was doing piano tuning for a concert at a big local conference. There was going to be a lot of different music being played there, from jazz and folk to classical, etc. There was a lot of focus on the kind of new age, spirituality, and awareness ideology. I met a guy named Neil who was the director of the event. He started asking me about how I got into the piano tuning trade and was very surprised that I tuned pianos by ear. I told him that I had a great vibrational connection, not only with my work but with life in general. Neil and I hit it off quickly, and after a lengthy conversation, he could see that we were wired very much the same. He said that my feelings and awareness of the Earth and Universe were what that event was all about. Neil asked me if I would be willing to give a lecture at the event since it was going to be a three-day festival. Neil also said that there was a last-minute opening because someone else had cancelled on him. He said to me, "I think you have a lot of knowledge and insight that people would gravitate towards," and that I would have the freedom to choose the topic I wanted. I agreed to do the lecture the last day of the event at 2 PM.

LECTURE ONE

It was now the final day of the event, a beautiful Sunday, and it was very crowded. I was not nervous at all because I had spent so much of my life on stage. In true Will Campbell fashion, I did not prepare the lecture and decided to wing it, like I had throughout my life. Shortly before 2 PM, Neil walked up on the stage and introduced me to the awaiting crowd. As I walked up on stage, I shook Neil's hand and thanked him. I then walked up to the podium to begin my lecture.

I raised my head and looked upon the crowd and, as I smiled, I said, just imagine yourself for a moment, sitting restlessly with a collectively anxious audience, awaiting the beautiful sounds of your favorite orchestra. You can hear a multitude of sounds, from people walking about to conversations back and forth, and even some distant laughter and various ambient noises. Suddenly, as the house lights begin to dim, the crowd noise subsides and begins to diminish. Off in the distance, from the side of the dark backstage, you can hear the soft footsteps as the maestro approaches the nine-foot black concert grand piano. The crowd erupts and graciously applauds the maestro. Soon a single spotlight captures her flowing red dress as she gives a slight bow and proceeds to sit down at the piano. Various stage lights begin to illuminate the beautiful setting as her hands approach the black-and-white piano keys. You can see her take a deep breath as she waits for the crowd noise to die down to a near silent hush. Suddenly, her hands rise as she begins to strike the first note of the concerto. As the white key depresses from her moderate blow, the hammer within the piano rises, striking the string to produce the vibration which will create the frequency of the beautiful note A. That note of A is followed by a melodic train of all the other notes soaring high above and out through the auditorium. The power of vibrating notes creates the frequencies and emotions that course through every single person in attendance. Collectively, everyone is completely focused on that magical moment. For a brief time in their lives, they are in total unison with each other. All this is due to the power of vibrations and their frequencies, beautifully crafted, allowing us to bond together as one living, breathing harmonious group.

I then told the crowd that this whole scene was something I could completely relate to, not only from a participant's standpoint, but also as someone who had spent a large portion of my life as a master piano technician. I told them that my wonderful career had given me a unique insight into the feelings of vibrations and frequencies that very few others could possibly perceive and comprehend. I suggested to everyone that similar scenarios could be played out under different settings. Perhaps a rock concert, starting with a guitar pick striking the first chord from the heavily distorted guitar strings. In turn, the guitar strings create vibrations which then send the frequencies to a wall of powerful Marshall amplifiers. Soon the drums, bass, and keyboards all kick in to the opening rock anthem. I said to them, imagine the concertgoers erupt in singing and screaming in unison, creating their own vibrations and frequencies. Once again, an extraordinary collective bond is formed by everyone in attendance.

I went on to say that perhaps we could look at another completely different setting, such as a hip-hop or rap concert that begins with the pulse of a beat from a single bass drum. It's then followed by the remaining heavy dance beats, creating a frenzy within the crowd. All those in attendance begin to move and dance and sing in unison. Here too, they are all united by not only their own movement, but all the vibrations and frequencies started with that single bass drumbeat. The energy connection that we all share at these events is undeniable, yet often overlooked, along with the amazing power it produces to really connect each one of us. In my opinion, I felt that music is the universal language worldwide, and I completely believed that to be true. There's nothing else like it on Earth. Music can bridge all gaps on a global level. It doesn't matter if it's political, religious, or any other forms that keep us separate from being one united, harmonious mankind.

I asked my audience to take a closer look at those things that we call vibrations and frequencies. It was a name given by our scientific interpretation of what we perceived them to be. I said, if you think about it, they are all around us. These vibrations are above us, to the left and to the right of us, as well as deep inside of us. Our world and beyond is immersed in vibrations and frequencies. I'm sure most people have never even thought about the sound of the vibrations and frequencies made by the tiny footsteps of an ant. How about the vibrations and frequencies from an unborn baby within the womb of a loving mother. Think about even smaller yet, all the way down to the vibrations created by swimming sperm, venturing toward an egg to create fertilization at the start of new life. Or perhaps the creaking of trees as they sway in the gentle breeze within a forest, with all its other sounds from vibration and frequencies. I asked those in attendance to allow themselves to drift off to our beautiful oceans and ponder about how many of them had heard or witnessed the thundering crash of a 65,000-pound humpback whale, leaping completely out of the water and rotating, then to finally land back in the water? I told them that the thundering crash from the whale's breach creates enormous vibrations and frequencies, sounding like a bomb going off. I asked, have you considered the possibility of hearing an earthquake and the rumbling vibrations and frequencies that shake our Earth, striking fear into all of us? I stated that the quake seems truly massive, but there's bigger even still. I asked, "Have you ever wondered, does the Earth itself make a sound?" I said to them, the truth is, the Earth does make a sound, and it has been measured, and it is called ambient seismic noise. That is the collective sound of the Earth's plates moving and shifting, along with all the other sounds and vibrations and their frequencies. Those sounds create our Earth's own monstrous collective universal sound.

I invited everyone there to take some moments in their life to find a peaceful place, wherever that may be, and if possible, go somewhere out in the beauty of nature. Go be still, I said to them, look and feel beyond what we normally see, hear, and sense. I asked my audience to let themselves be totally connected with what we call the universe. While doing this, allow yourself to understand that everything living and nonliving, not only in our world but universally, is connected through vibrational frequencies. I remarked that it all goes much deeper than that, even if you allow yourself to consider that thoughts and emotions and senses too are all connected the same way. Look at how our modern technology has stunted our emotional and primal connection to the Earth and the universe. Our ego has convinced us that we are so advanced. However, I feel in many ways, it is very infantile compared to past ancient civilizations. We have disconnected with the vibrational flow of Mother Earth and everything around us. For as far as we've come into our own minds, for many of us, our eyes are like a newborn baby. Our eyes are not yet opened to see the true picture. We really seem to be missing the process of what the life we are all given is, and then much farther beyond that. Our current technology also gives us a false sense of knowing and disconnects us from those primal senses. I said that everything else on this Earth is connected primally because every living, breathing second is based on new life and survival. Every other form of life has a constant awareness of what's around them so that they can produce new life and protect it. Also, these other life forms focus on passing on the knowledge and understanding of the Earth before their time has passed and they have moved on to other dimensions. So much of what various lifeforms on this planet perceive causes them to make calculated choices every second. This is done through some form of connection with vibrational frequencies. How connected are you or me, I asked? That is something that we all need to explore more. Our eyes need to open like the newborn infant, possibly seeing clearly for the first time what is the true gift of our own lives.

I beckoned my captive audience to look at something that I referred to as non-conforming animals. I said, if we take a deeper look into all life on this planet, we will see that every living, breathing life form, from our largest that we know of, the blue whale, all the way down to an enormous variety of microscopic organisms, all share similar experiences. Whether their life lasts for a minute or a hundred years, how they breathe, move, eat, or how they reproduce is connected by vibrational frequencies. Also, how they survive until they eventually die and pass on is connected the same way. I told them that in life there is movement, and when you have movement, even at the slowest pace, there is vibration created from it. Those vibrations in turn then create various frequencies. So, everything is tied together by that which some call the circle of life. Well, all the life on this planet accepts its place in the circle and lives and dies, even if violent, with harmony and balance. There is one animal that does not. Unfortunately, as humans, we are the only ones not living in total harmony and balance with everything else. As we look further back into our own history, you don't have to go too far to find people who did try their best to live in balance. The Native American Indians and various other primal cultures throughout the world certainly did that for a very long time. They understood this balance and I believe also understood the connection between vibration and frequency to Mother Earth. Unfortunately, I said, we have become so lost over time that we have lost sight of that true connection. So many people on the planet are unable to recognize it, let alone believe that it even exists. Sadly, I feel that this blindness is a great detriment to our survival as a species. One thing I do know is that the Earth has been cycling for billions of years. It will continue to do so, even at the cost of wiping out that which is not in compliance.

I looked deeply at the audience there and said that there were many people throughout the world who do believe we are out of balance. Some even suggest that climate change is to blame for things not being what they used to be. I'm not here to debate any political side of the spectrum or any so-called conspiracy theories out there. However, if we really look at the Earth over vast amounts of time, we can easily see how weather patterns and how everything associated with that cycle is very different from times long ago. Our Earth and the universe have always been changing. Living harmoniously within our own planet is something that we seem to struggle with as a species. If we look at weather patterns throughout many years, modern scientists have only been able to study it for about one hundred and fifty years. That's just a tiny speck in time. People tend to forget just how different things were very long ago on our planet. For instance, Greenland was not always cold, and neither was the Arctic. The Earth's axis has been shifted several times over millions of years from catastrophic events, which changed the poles of the Earth. Then, weather patterns changed drastically too. Our overall vibrational harmony is overlooked by us. I believe the Earth continues, as it always must, to cycle and change and will return to what it may have been long ago. For those people who are hung up on the politics of climate change and those ideas, I don't believe any political party on either side or anywhere in the world is going to change it. It's a nice talking point perhaps, but in the end, our Earth will continue to cycle as it always has. I believe that as a species we all need to become more vibrationally connected. I think that it's important for us to focus deeper within ourselves on a personal level. We must see our own mind, body, and spirit as our own personal universe and try to live as best we can in balance. Maybe then, as a collective species throughout the world, we can once again learn to live in vibrational harmony, just as our great ancestors did long ago. I then thanked my wonderful audience for listening.

After my lecture, I received a warming round of applause. As I left the stage, many people approached me to thank me and asked where I might be speaking again. I was very gracious with them and said I'm not sure but please keep an eye out for me. Neil had made his way through the crowd and very excitedly thanked me and asked me if I would be interested in giving lectures at other events around the region. I told Neil that I would love to if I could have the flexibility to change up the topics. He said he had complete faith in me and that I had freedom to go with my instincts. The next upcoming event was a month away, and I was excited about it. Once again, I would not prepare anything. I would just speak from my heart and soul.

LECTURE TWO

The next event was about two hours from my home. It was a beautiful Friday afternoon, and it was already crowded. My start time was the same, 2 p.m. I met Neil again, and we briefly chatted before the lecture. Neil asked if I had any notes, and I just laughed. I told him that my overall message would be similar, just delivered a little differently. He said, "I have no doubt things will go smoothly." Once again, Neil introduced me as Will Campbell to the audience. I walked up on the stage, thanked Neil for having me, and then thanked the crowd for sharing their time with me.

I began my lecture and said, "Know thyself sounds like an ancient phrase, and indeed it is. Basically, it's just the process of self-awareness or a process of being. It's quite simple when you break it down; it stands the test of time for all generations. The truth is that it is something that is severely overlooked by most people. The phrase, 'know thyself' means exactly what it says— and that is to completely understand your whole self. To do this, we as humans must look deep within ourselves on a very basic, fundamental, vibrational level. Maybe even try to reach a very deep, multilayered view of ourselves and our past selves. We all have different purposes within our present life that we are currently walking in, and sometimes our purposes are developed more as we go along. Those purposes can also be quite flexible throughout the short period that we are given in our present life here on Earth. Much of who we are, as we look at ourselves today, is greatly influenced by a combination of who we were in our previous lives, even going way back to ancient times. The journey is very different for everyone, and unfortunately, most people are just completely stuck in the little mental box that they currently live in. They don't even get to see the full potential for the present form of life that they are in now, let alone allow themselves to look at their past selves. Perhaps we should attempt to look and see who we may have been in the past and what has forged us into being what we recognize in our current form. People need to stop and look at all the subtleties that make up who they are. Until we can begin to recognize and feel things from long ago that got us to where we are today, we will be lost without a complete sense of self. Many people struggle to feel or see deep feelings or thoughts within themselves, like, 'I may have been here before,' or 'I may have done this before.' Imagine yourself thinking that it's no surprise that you are heading in the direction of a career or just everyday life. Perhaps we should ponder our many life choices, like people we meet, people we date, or people we marry. All these things we do in life are finely connected through vibrational energy and joined on the universal plane that we all share. Even how we interact with people, our careers, nature, animals, and everything around us are directly influenced partly by our deep subconscious self. That deep part of our being is greatly overlooked or missed by most people. I told my audience: don't think for a second that your interest in music, fine art, or any other great skills you may have in life has not, in some way or another, been influenced by a deep form of a past you. We are meant to adapt and mold and evolve in the present life that we are currently living in. I also believe that holds true for what you could call the long game. All those lives that we have been blessed with—and will be in our future lives as well— are all profoundly vibrationally connected. I understand and accept that there will be those who criticize my thoughts because they may challenge what might be considered normal, conventional reasoning. However, we must be true to all that we feel and perceive around us in the past, present, and the future. I asked the crowd to just look at all you do and all you believe, and you will see that some of your tendencies have been with you for a very long time. I feel that there is beauty in being able to recognize our past. I also firmly believe that it will help forge our future, how we evolve and how or who we become tomorrow and beyond.

I told everyone there that we've seen countless slip-ups in history from radical world leaders and the people that follow them, because they don't recognize the past and some of the mistakes that have been made on a basic human level. So, the result is continued failure and even a spiritual backslide as a society. Too often we have not learned from the wrong forks in the road that we walked down. Going down the wrong road without recognizing and learning from our mistakes just keeps us repeating the same tasks before us until we get it right. This has been a pattern throughout not only the history we know but also the ancient history we have forgotten. I said I always reflect on the teachings and inspiring words of my dad Ed. One saying of his always stands out in my mind. He would say, "Just because someone says it so, does not make it so." That is really an incredibly powerful statement—and profoundly true. Often, we listen to or read various types of information, lectures, propaganda, or watch TV, or engage in various forms of social media, etc. We often completely believe what is being delivered to us. We see so many people spewing opinions all over the place and often coming across as very authoritative with those opinions. As strong and authoritative as their statements may be, it is not always so, as my father Ed would say. Even historically, there have been great manipulators in various religious organizations, cults, or politics, including world leaders. They can disrupt our positive vibrational flow of energy. The true masters of manipulation can deliver those warped and twisted messages so strongly and so convincingly that people gravitate to them. The blinded followers believe the false message with all their hearts and souls. In some cases, they may follow it—even to the detriment and harm or even death of themselves or others. The true masters of manipulation can convince people that they are supposedly justified in those false radical ideals. The list of these mind pirates that steal what is considered normal reasoning from legions of followers is very long, historically. I told the audience that I was speaking in a historical broad sense, not necessarily of specific current times. I reiterate to them that this was not political grandstanding but an attempt to suggest that we try to make the best decisions for ourselves as we journey down our current road of life. The common sense behind my father's statement was quite simple. It basically was just telling people to really reflect on what they hear from outside sources. Take the time to really look deep within ourselves and analyze those things with as level a head as possible. If we trust our gut, so to speak, the truth and honesty will shine through and weed out the misinformation, the type of misinformation that could lead us down a bad path of harm and destruction. I believe strongly in our instincts, as did my dad. It's not always a perfect mechanism, but it is surely a good filter if we use it properly. We all need to put more emphasis on our deep feelings and connect with the deep, wise, vibrational past within all of us. At the end of the day, I ask you to use your filter and trust your gut and judgment—not only on what I have to say, but on anything anyone else has to say to you.

I told my audience that politics and religion are the two prime examples of extreme exaggeration used to push an agenda, whatever that might be. Behind all those organizations lies one single thing—and that is always power. Power is like the ultimate drug! Worse than booze or any other form of narcotics. It steers us away from common sense thinking and control within our own lives. Power is intoxicating to those who seek it, and it builds upon itself. A warped sense of power is like a bad pyramid scheme. Negative power disturbs the positive flow of energy within all of us. The creator behind the warped sense of power shares his or her views with a few people initially. Then they, in turn, share those views—once they are manipulated—with a few more people. Quickly, on it goes, just like a corrupt multi-level marketing scheme. Suddenly it goes from one psycho sense of reality to thousands of people having a psychotic break and wholeheartedly believing in all that they are pushing! This can be potentially dangerous for all of us if not disqualified. "Know thyself" is something we can all become more aware of, as we allow ourselves to be more in touch with our own ancient selves. By doing so, deep vibrational information within us—that feels right or wrong— will emerge to guide us. Take time to analyze and really think about what you hear every given day. Carefully allow yourself to digest it and then make the best decision you can. Always remember that just because someone says it so, does not make it so.

I said to my dear friends in attendance, most of us are caught on the hamster wheel of life. Unfortunately, we keep going around, running feverishly in our busy routines like a horse wearing blinders. We usually can only see what is in front of us and are completely missing the big picture all around us. We are probably more disconnected in our lives now than ever, particularly in our family groups. We've all been out at a restaurant, or a family gathering and glanced across the room and saw our dysfunction. Like when we are all staring down at our cell phones, having absolutely no interaction between us, other than the technology that we have become a slave to. It's very unfortunate, and I feel that as a society, we will pay a high price for this disconnection down the road. The smartphone is probably the greatest technological achievement and advancement in our modern history. It has unfortunately completely removed us from a lot of normal social interaction. We are not paying attention to the vibrational flow that we are all connected to. We are completely bombarded as a society by so much clutter and outside sources such as TVs, phones, computers, etc. Consider taking time for silence and meditation and allowing the true sounds of the Earth to be absorbed by you and your soul. Imagine just turning the TV off one day and all the other outside noise and getting away from the cell phone and the computer. Maybe you will be able to hear that bird chirping outside your window. Imagine now going for a nice quiet stroll in a park or, if you're blessed to live in a quiet neighborhood, just taking in the sounds around you. Some of the best times are at dusk when things truly start to quiet and the nightlife creeps in. Imagine again listening to the trees as they sway in the breeze or the sound of a hawk screeching high above us. Wouldn't it be beautiful to walk by a quiet stream and really listen to the stream as it goes by, as it gives life to all around it? Maybe then we can start listening to wildlife while they're making their own unique sounds, communicating with each other and the Earth. The only thing missing from the picture is us connected with them. Together let's make a deeper effort to look beyond the obvious and maybe finally see the whole beautifully interconnected vibrational scene before us. Dear people, I said, as I see it, most people go through life blinded and only accept what they see before them or what they've been taught and programmed to know. Many religions around the globe teach their followers to believe in a higher being and trust in what they can't see. They are instructed that the supreme being or God is always with them, watching over them. Their true followers will believe undeniably in what they've been taught, even if they can't see or touch it. I too accept this form of teaching, but in a bit more vibrational, spiritual way. I challenge you to look deeper and harder inside of yourself at every step in life. It is my belief that you can see and feel things that connect us with a higher life force, including the Earth and all those vibrational connections and senses that most of us lost long ago.

I invited the crowd to consider something called the fish test. It is a simple challenge, and I said that some of you may even know this theory. Consider walking past a beautiful stream, and you come upon a pool with many life forms and beautiful fish right there that you can see from the bank. This is the perfect example of two dimensions right before your eyes that are clearly separated—for you and the fish. You cannot live in the fish's world, and he cannot live in yours. You can see each other; you can feel each other's vibrations of movement if you are aware of it—but there is a clear separation. Seriously, to the fish you may as well be on planet Mars. You're both right there, yet so far apart—and yet still so connected. Well, that is until he bites on your line, and you reel him in and welcome him to Mars! The crowd laughed a bit, and I said you get the idea here; it's a simple lesson but one we can all relate to. All those things are so close and very vibrationally connected on a universal level, and they are right in front of our eyes—but seemingly so distant from each other. What else is right in front of all of us, yet separated by another dimension that most of us have quite possibly lost the ability to see? Countless unusual or unexplained things have been sighted all over the world for centuries. Could it be that maybe some of these unexplained sights are merely something slipping through, possibly for a glimpse from another dimension that exists right alongside us? Maybe awakening some of our long-lost senses will unlock an enhanced form of sight or a knowing that will reconnect us vibrationally with other possible dimensions. Just like ourselves and the fish—we are both right there together, but at the same time infinitely separated.

I said that quiet times in peace and serenity is like getting your batteries recharged. Just take time to allow nature's vibrational energy into your soul instead of walking around angry at the world over trivial things. Often, complete serenity can be as good as it gets and all we really need to see clearly. What a shame it is to miss out on those things when they're right there for all of us to enjoy. I urge all of you to embrace those quiet moments when you can, and I assure you it will be grounding and positive for you. Always believe in your deep inner instincts. Remember, life is good, life is hopeful, and life and nature are a gift to all of us. Embrace it all, and maybe then we can see how our souls are eternally vibrationally connected with the Earth and universe. As I closed, I looked upon the audience and said, thank you for your time, and I wish all of you a peaceful and wonderful day.

I received warm, appreciative applause after my second lecture. I had the opportunity to meet so many kind and like-minded people. Neil informed me that the next lecture was a bit further away, about four hours driving. He said that he was sorry that they could not compensate me for my time. Maybe they could bump up the ticket prices to generate some money for me. I said that was not necessary at all. I didn't expect any payment, and it was an honor to speak and spend time with so many wonderful people. I shook Neil's hand and said, "I'll see you at the next event."

LECTURE THREE

The next event was at a beautiful outdoor setting nestled in the woods on the grounds of an unexpected rare American castle. As usual, Neil introduced me, and I could sense that people started to know who I was, and they came to listen to my lecture. It was very heartwarming as I took the stage with enthusiastic, wonderful applause.

I began my lecture again and said, welcome friends to this magnificent, beautiful, and enchanting setting. As we go through our everyday activities and through our bigger journey in life, we run mindlessly and do all sorts of things. We must go here, must run there, it's just an endless cycle of busyness for many of us. We think to ourselves that we have so much time, especially since we expect to live what we perceive to be a long and fulfilling life. Could it be that we humans are just like a fly? That may seem a bit perplexing, since many of us have not had much love for the little flies. To most of us, flies tend to be rather pesky, to say the least. Like everything else around us in life, even flies have their purpose in nature and the universe. They are very much vibrationally connected to Mother Earth and our universal circle. In fact, a fly's life task is crucial; yet most of us are unaware of their critical role. Flies have been on our planet for roughly two hundred and sixty million years! They serve an extremely important role on our planet, because only second to bees, flies are the top pollinators in the world. Also, because their longevity has been so great on this planet, they are most likely responsible for the early pollination on the Earth millions of years ago. So why do I mention flies, of all things, to all of you? If you ask most people, how long do flies live? I'll bet the top response that you will get is three days. The truth is that most fly species only live about a month, and some rare species live up to a year. Will, how does this affect me, you may ask? Well, the reason I bring them up is quite simple indeed. Since they do truly have a short life cycle, imagine all that needs to be done and experienced by a fly within that short period of time. Flies know their role in nature, and they play it perfectly. Perhaps we as humans are quite like the fly after all. Maybe our existence, and what we contribute, and what we're learning and passing on to our offspring, is merely just a blip on the universal radar. Just as the fly's life cycle is considered a mere blip, so is our own oh-so-important life cycle.

I asked the audience to try for one second to set aside our big, bloated, egotistical mindset as a human race. Maybe we could even allow ourselves to possibly consider how we sit in the cosmos, or within the history of our planet—or what we think is the history of our planet. Well, I say that it is we who are that annoying little fly racing around and trying to get oh so much done in such a short time, before our crucial little life cycle comes to an end. We are truly only here for a very short amount of time, in terms of how we have defined time in our own existence. There is still a lot of history being taught that the current human, as we know it, only goes back a few thousand years. The truth is that not too long ago, we found evidence that it goes back more than ten thousand years. Every year, all around the globe, we are uncovering more in our ancient history that keeps pushing our human history further back, shattering the current historical theories as we know them to be. We think we know our own history, but we haven't got a clue, or we're just too close-minded to accept the fact that we have been here for eons. Quite possibly, some other form of us—or some other completely different type of life form altogether—was here on our planet long ago. Maybe our ancient predecessors were highly intelligent and capable of doing all kinds of amazing things that we cannot do even now. I believe there has been intelligent life on this planet not only hundreds of thousands of years but possibly going back much further than that—possibly even millions of years. Quite frankly, after about one thousand years, the chance of any evidence other than rock surviving is slim. Almost any trace of ancient civilizations would be gone, unless buried deep in the earth or under the oceans and glaciers. With our own advancing technologies, we are slowly uncovering small pieces of our ancient history here on Earth. I fully believe that our ancient ancestors were very much vibrationally connected to the Earth and the universe. I believe they understood that connection and quite possibly were able to harness the energetic forces for the advancement of their current technology. Perhaps it was far greater than anything we can comprehend. However, I'll bet that they too were possibly zooming through their own short life in the cosmos. So fast forward to our time now, and just like little flies, we race around within our expected lifespan, a tiny fraction in time, which is nothing in the big scheme of things. We are just so determined to say that we have it all figured out and that we know our own history. We assume that everything we're doing right now is just so critically important to the planet. I say we need to set our huge egos aside, because we are just the little fly! Because we are here for such a small period, we do not control the bigger realm or the long game of the history of our planet. The fly is in acceptance and compliance with the vibrational universe; however, we are not. Think about the little fly, I said, and just ponder it on a universal vibrational level. Then really think about all we know about us and what we don't know yet. Our personal existence here on Earth and what we call the universe is no more than what the fly's existence is to us.

I then said to the audience, I would like to talk to you about a topic that many of us share in some way or another. I will preface this by saying that this is not meant to be an endorsement or a condemnation of anyone's religious beliefs. I'll bet if I asked any of you, how many religions do you think are currently in the world? My guess is most of you would say between one hundred to two hundred religions are currently practiced globally. The true rough calculations, if you Google how many religions are in the world, is a stunning answer. The number is not exact, but approximately four thousand two hundred religions are currently recognized worldwide! What's even more fascinating about that statistic, other than the large number, is that all of them have one thing in common. They all believe that they are the path to salvation—or what is defined as salvation by their own criteria. I want you to think about that for a moment, it's truly astounding. Somewhere in that thought process, somebody must be wrong, because they all surely can't be right. If we locate just the top religions globally, you will find some similarities behind the fundamentals of how they all operate. They are all based on being a better human being and on living by a set of rules set forth by the said religion. This within itself is not a bad thing, because I do believe we need structure and guidelines to keep us on track in a chaotic world. It helps us eliminate the chance of becoming out of control with no rules. Also, most of the religions—even back to ancient times—carry a common theme. With all of them, the so-called god or gods descended from above and gave us knowledge and guidelines as to how we should survive and live to the fullest in the eyes of those gods. Those religions were developed thousands of miles apart, many years ago. Remarkably, they all had such similar backgrounds in the stories of gods coming down from the heavens. They also had similar stories of a great catastrophic event which wiped out humanity—or basically was a restart for mankind as well.

I believe our ancient predecessors were much higher and greater civilizations that lived here long ago, even going back hundreds of thousands of years or more. I also believe that they were annihilated by cataclysmic events or great wars here on Earth, and that we did have possibly multiple restarts of civilization. Much of the ancient technology and ideology was lost long ago, and what remained may not have been allowed to be taught because it would inherently interfere with the narrative or agendas of our modern religions. Over time, religions would splinter off from each other for mostly political reasons or some ideological differences within the members. Basically, some splintering factions would take what they wanted out of a particular religion and then mold in their own politics to what suited them better. The new emerging religion would preach that new doctrine to the masses that would follow them, and then so on and so on down the road they would go. This is the very reason why we have so many religions today. They are all claiming to be the one and the only path to what we call eternity or salvation. Believe it or not, there is really a religion called the Church of the Flying Spaghetti Monster. Its members are called Pastafarians, which is rather humorous. However, there are thousands of members around the world. The religion is satirical in nature, and it was created to mock traditional religious dogma and structure. I have a very simple and humorous way of explaining how this can happen, and I call it Johnnyism.

My theory goes like this: a group of people are hanging out late one evening and they are having a typical Friday night party with some alcohol and various drugs. One guy named Johnny is sitting in the corner, drunk and high, when suddenly he has an incredible cerebral epiphany! Johnny's little intoxicated brain opens and coincidentally has some amazing revelations. These thoughts come through because he has reached a higher state of consciousness and doesn't even understand where his spirit has landed, but he's having a great time and loving this wild, amazing trip. Johnny starts to blurt out a few profound statements—or what he perceives them to be. The other stoners and drunks in the room soon begin to think that Johnny is onto something truly special. Meanwhile, Johnny is still tripping and does not even realize that they are all overwhelmed by his so-called profound babble. Johnny is a likable guy, and he just continues to spout out what he hears or sees in his open trippy mind. Suddenly Johnny is being elevated and put on a pedestal by everyone in the room. They all declare that Johnny is really onto something, and they need to cultivate and treasure this abundance of remarkable proclamations. Without Johnny even realizing it, he's swiftly anointed to the head of this new and incredible thought process. Better yet, who better to be his selected closest followers than those in the room that were blown away by those incredible proclamations. There we have it, ladies and gentlemen, the seeds of a new religion have been planted. Before you know it, one of the stoners anoints him a prophet, and boom—just like that, a new religion is born. Johnnyism, in honor of their great new leader! Before long, Johnny is thrust into his new role and starts to take his own proclamations seriously. Everyone says, man, we've got to spread the word. Off go the stoner disciples to the high schools or jobs or wherever else they are branching out into. They now feel it's their purpose to let other people know that this guy Johnny is really something special. You all need to come hear him speak, they say! Then, as they continue to spread all his glorious words more, it gets even bigger. More stoners and more boozers and lots of people who need something to gravitate to in their empty lives show up and drink the Johnny-flavored Kool-Aid. Many of the suddenly infected idiots proclaim, oh my god, this guy is the real deal! So, this new can of religious goodies is kicked down the road, and as it rolls, it picks up more and more mindless followers, and eventually they figure hey, we can make some money at this too! Next, the brilliant, empowered stoners set up some rules and guidelines and of course start collecting contributions! Oh my, we can even be tax-free—in fact, a nonprofit organization. Let's not forget that our gracious leader Johnny deserves all the best things in life. He deserves a great car, a spiffy new castle to live in as well, and all the comforts of any great leader. Oh, and of course all his closest followers from the beginning will be taken care of too, because they were the initial believers, spreading the word like a plague to all the lost souls. After quite some time, Johnny is fully embedded in his own delusions. Everything that he says is deemed the truth and the way to eternal salvation. Over even more time, generations after generations continue the process set forth by their exalted lord stoner Johnny.

Well, my friends, I said, I by no means am criticizing religions. I think that they have, for the most part, a good foundation and basis for people to follow. However, I also believe that much of how the universe really works is completely lost and surely not reinforced by any of those religions. If any of our current religious organizations dared to talk about our true ancient history, all their theories and narratives would be shot, and they would have no reason for existence. This is not to say that all the founders of religions are stoners and boozers—it's just a humorous example of how it can happen and how some of them have really happened. I accept the belief that there were many true so-called prophets in history, but I also believe that they were just able to truly tap into what is referred to as an awakening within our higher self. Their interpretations of these awakenings, no matter how profound or ridiculous, formed the basis of the various religions for them and their future followers. The answers that we all so desperately search for from a spiritual, religious, or higher self-aspect in life can all be found if we take time to be still and listen to our inner vibrational voice. Then we must all go even deeper and really listen within that silence. I believe that there, in that silence, we too will be able to be truly connected with this great world and the universe that we are all so fortunate to be a part of.

Another topic that I would like to share with everyone is called Tribal Divide. The world as we know it today is made up of very different cultural, ethnic, and even religious groups that separate us in many ways. In fact, that division has been that way for a very long time. This tribal divide keeps us vibrationally disconnected from each other and, more importantly, from Mother Earth. As you look back in time, you will also clearly see all the separations of humanity. We regretfully have never been fully united on a global level that we know of.

I recently watched a popular TV series with my wife Gwen one evening. I commented to her that all those people do in the show is have sex and kill each other over various power struggles within that northern European region. Anyone that follows the show knows that there is a giant struggle between the various clans. It's all over who will rule the various kingdoms or what they perceive as their world. In the show, they are broken up into various clans from similar ethnic backgrounds, within one culture. The truth is, we are no different today than we were centuries ago. Everything is just on a global scale now, and we are still broken into various tribes. We still suffer from a vibrational disconnect and continue to have the same types of separations, including some politics and religion sprinkled in. These divisions within our nations, or tribes around the world, are the one thing that keeps us all from being unified. It's a shame that the ego of all of us is what separates our tribes and destroys any chance of unity between all of us. It would be very difficult for any one person around the world to honestly say that there are no divisional separations, whether it be religious, cultural, political, or whatever, between you and someone else. Even the best of us will have some form of division if we are truly being honest with ourselves. How can we attain vibrational harmony and become globally unified? I really think it would have to take some huge global event to even have a sliver of a chance to bring us all truly together. Maybe someday, as we continue our space explorations and move off beyond our planet through technological development, we may have a chance to unify. Perhaps at that point, we will have to look at ourselves as one vibrationally connected tribe here on Mother Earth.

Recently, while listening to the classic song *Imagine* by John Lennon, it was obvious what he was writing about, but as we truly look at the picture, it was so far from reality. We have spent eons developing a thought process within our tribes. It is extremely difficult for us to deprogram ourselves and to look at everything as a unit instead of how we are different. Unfortunately, I feel that religion and politics are the biggest wedges that separate all our tribes. It's such a sad reality, especially since I find most religions to be highly hypocritical. They often spew a false narrative of unity and inclusiveness, yet they reject and condemn all those who disagree with the doctrine that they have dictated as righteous. I will admit that I am tribally separated too, for various reasons. A big part of me longs for global unity, but then often those old tribal influences creep in and set me back. It's basically all the usual programming that most of us are indoctrinated with, particularly when we are young, and often we find it difficult to fully shake it off. I frequently must check my own personal views of tribes different than my own as well. Most importantly, if we can catch ourselves in a moment of weakness and see beyond our divisions, then we can progress in the right direction. I hope that as we all grow through life, that we can tear down some of these walls that have been imprinted on us throughout not only our lifetime but the generations before us and after us. It's an extremely difficult task, but not an impossibility, and hopefully one day our future generations will be able to reach this monumental goal. Keep in mind, I said to the crowd, we are all connected vibrationally on a deep underlying current, but most will never recognize the common thread between all of us. As for now, we can only try to change little things within ourselves to build steppingstones to a better inclusive mindset. Hopefully, that will move us toward this global unification, and like the song says, for now we will have to *imagine*. I then said to my beautiful audience: thank you for listening, and let's keep peace and love within all our hearts.

For a third time, I was fortunate to have gracious applause from the audience. As usual, Neil shook my hand and thanked me. He said they were going to be taking some time off with the tour but resuming later in the year around the country. Neil said that he would stay in touch with me moving forward. With that, we parted and went our separate ways. I was very grateful for the opportunity to share my thoughts with so many wonderful people. My partial retirement and future looked hopeful, and off again I went forward on my own journey in the fourth quarter of my life.

16

THE WHISPERING

I t had been quite some time since any mysterious or dark type of presence had presented itself to me. Life had settled into a peaceful rhythm. I went about my days working on pianos, keeping my hands busy with repairs, tunings, and all my various home projects and hobbies. Things were calm, ordinary—almost deceptively so. Of course, me being the very open creature that I was, unusual things were never completely off the table. They had a way of showing up, quietly, unannounced, waiting until just the right moment. For the most part, I dealt with things that came through to me as best I could throughout my life. But I could feel it in the background—that thin hum beneath the silence. Once again, I would experience another unusual presence, this time while in a higher vibrational state of consciousness that seemed to arrive when I least expected it.

While I was out on the road working one afternoon, I received a phone call from a long-term piano client named Max. Max was a retired undertaker and served as a choir director at a local church. His voice on the phone always carried a strange calmness, almost as if he were still speaking from some shadowed corner of a dimly lit funeral parlor. That day, he asked if I'd be willing to take on a new client named Joe—a friend of his and, coincidentally, another undertaker. I said of course, just have him call me. Max said Joe was very busy and that he'd make the arrangements himself. We agreed on a 2 PM piano tuning at Joe's house. Max told me Joe would be there to meet me.

When I arrived at the appointment, to my surprise, it was Max who opened the door. His expression was unusually blank. He stepped aside and said calmly, "Joe had a heart attack last night."

That stopped me for a moment.

"He's in the hospital—doing relatively okay," Max added. "But he insisted the piano still get tuned."

I nodded, stepping into the dimly lit house. The air was thick with the scent of age—dry wood, mildew, and something else I couldn't quite name. Max told me Joe's funeral parlor was two houses down, and that he usually had eight or nine bodies there at any given time. That image stuck in my mind like a thorn.

Joe's house matched his profession perfectly: a creaky old Victorian that could've passed for a haunted boarding house in some forgotten town. The paint was faded, windows tall and arched, the atmosphere steeped in quiet tension. I knew right away the piano hadn't been tuned in ages—it would need a pitch correction. That's a two-step process: the first day brings it close to the standard pitch; the second visit locks everything in.

While I worked through the initial tuning, Max informed me he couldn't stay and prepaid me for both visits. With that, he left the house. Alone, I continued working, feeling the weight of the stillness around me. Every creak in the floorboards seemed to echo. I packed up, finished my work, and carried on with the rest of my day.

The following week, I headed back for the second tuning. On the way, I called Max to let him know I was running a bit behind. He said he wouldn't be there this time, but Joe's wife would let me in. That seemed simple enough.

When I arrived and knocked on the door, it swung open—and there was Joe himself. Pale, thin, and stiff in posture, he smiled and said hello in a voice that didn't quite match the expression. I was stunned. He had just suffered a heart attack a few days earlier and now stood before me as though nothing had happened.

I introduced myself and asked how he was feeling.

"Doing well," he said. "Only a mild one."

I nodded slowly, then went to the piano. It was a dusty old grand piano tucked into the corner of a parlor that hadn't seen sunlight in some time. Joe mentioned the piano was over a hundred years old and had once lived in the funeral parlor before being relocated to his home. That fact alone made the hairs on my arms stand up. Objects carry energy. Pianos, especially those in spiritually charged places, tend to soak up the room's vibrations over time.

Joe walked over to a worn chair across the room and sat down, arms crossed. I didn't get good energy from him, nothing concrete, but an intuitive resistance, a strange tension in his posture and presence. Then my phone locked up. I couldn't access anything, not even the home screen. I rebooted it twice, and it still wouldn't cooperate.

I've always been aware that spiritual energies, especially lingering ones, can disrupt electronic devices. It's not something you can prove, but when you've lived with that sensitivity for years, you know. You feel it. I had the strong suspicion that my phone would work just fine once I was outside and away from whatever was surrounding me now.

Not long after, Joe's wife and daughter entered the room. They seemed kind and welcoming. We exchanged brief pleasantries, and they joined Joe across the room, chatting softly. I kept working, but something in the room was shifting.

A creeping unease started moving in around me. Not loud. Not obvious. Just a subtle change in the air—thicker, colder, like the barometric pressure had suddenly dropped. That kind of change you feel more than see. I couldn't shake the feeling that something—or someone—was watching me. I'd been in many strange homes over the years, but this had a uniquely oppressive quality to it.

Then, while I was moving up the chromatic scale tuning each note, something strange happened.

I heard a voice. Very faint. Very nearby. Whispering.

At first, I thought it was part of the conversation across the room. But the voice wasn't coming from their direction. It was inside my left ear—soft, slow, and female. Whispering the note names with me, in time, as I tuned.

C… C-sharp… D… D-sharp…

It was unnerving. I snapped my head around toward Joe. He remained seated, engaged in quiet conversation. No one in the room was acknowledging what I was hearing. It was just me.

The whispering continued.

And yet, I didn't sense malice. It was eerie, yes—absolutely—but not threatening. There was something deeply sad, almost tender about the voice. I had the distinct feeling this presence belonged to someone long passed—possibly someone who once played or cherished the piano. A woman, perhaps, whose energy was still attached.

I said nothing aloud. In my mind, I whispered back, Hello… I hear you.

The energy softened, though the whispers never stopped.

I tuned through the last few notes with deliberate care, listening to both the instrument and the spirit echoing behind it. When I finished, I turned to the family, smiled politely, and thanked them. They remained unaware of anything unusual. I didn't mention the whispering. How could I?

As I stepped through the door, I smiled once more and, in my mind, I said goodbye to my whispering friend.

I slid into my car, closed the door—and like clockwork, my phone turned on perfectly, as if nothing had happened.

Driving away, I shook my head and chuckled softly at myself. These experiences would never stop. Strange, unexplained phenomena had followed me throughout my life. I didn't go looking for them—they came to me. And I had long since made peace with that.

Still, I thought about that whisper. The timing, the location, the history of the piano—it all added up to something more than just imagination. That was the kind of vibrational connection I often found myself tapped into. A subtle gift. One that walked a fine line between insight and haunting.

And in that moment, with the afternoon sun breaking through the clouds and lighting the road ahead, I reminded myself of something I always held close: If I remain open—quietly receptive—then even the whispers of the forgotten might find their way through.

17

VIBRATIONS KEY TO IT ALL

I continued my lectures, and I began to gain a bit of notoriety around the country. My talks began to attract a curious blend of souls—seekers, wanderers, skeptics turned believers, and even those who simply felt the need to be somewhere they couldn't quite explain. My lectures always included my deep vibrational connection through my piano tuning career, which had become more than just a profession—it had become a sacred art, a spiritual gateway. Through those delicate adjustments of tone and resonance, I found a language that spoke beyond words, a connection to something greater. I continued sharing my spiritual ideas with all the beautiful souls across America, always speaking from the heart, raw and real. Because I was in my sixties, all my life experiences and regressions had ripened into a profound awareness. They allowed me to see with an inner clarity, to better understand the subtleties I had always felt and sensed but could never fully explain until now.

Vibrations are what I always believed to be the essential thread running through the fabric of existence. Not just here on this planet, but out into the farthest reaches of the universe. Everything around us, every object, every being, every thought, carries a unique vibrational frequency. It's as if the cosmos is singing an eternal, intricate symphony. There are vibrational forces that exist far beyond our comprehension, echoing through our solar system, pulsing through galaxies we've never seen, whispering across dimensions. Though we've made incredible strides in telescopic science, allowing us to glimpse the edge of creation, what we can see is still limited, a grain of sand on an infinite beach. But vibration—sound—has the ability to travel, to permeate, to slip through the invisible boundaries of space and time. Radio frequencies, born of these vibrations, pass effortlessly through barriers—cosmic dust, meteor belts, gravitational waves. They hum their eternal messages across the galaxies. Sound and vibrational energy are truly miraculous. Their potential is vast, mysterious, and still largely unknown to our limited human awareness.

Yet despite these truths, mankind's ego continues to blind us. It binds so many in the arrogant belief that we, humans, are the pinnacle of all life. That we are somehow the sole intelligent species in this magnificent, boundless universe is a notion so laughable, so painfully narrow-minded, it hardly deserves the dignity of rebuttal. We are but specks in a sea of stars, and yet we crown ourselves as kings. Every year, we unearth new truths—buried cities, sunken monuments, hidden temples beneath oceans—whispers from the ancients who came before us. These discoveries suggest that we are not the beginning of intelligent life here, but rather the continuation, perhaps even a rebuilding. Evidence mounts that great civilizations existed long before us—thriving, advanced societies whose wisdom was lost to time. Look at the pyramids, Stonehenge, and other monuments whose creation defies our modern capabilities. Many believe they were built with technologies now forgotten—technologies rooted in the manipulation of sound and vibration. And still, modern scholars scoff. Their egos cannot allow for truths that challenge their textbooks. But I believe these civilizations go back hundreds of thousands of years, maybe more, shattering the tidy timelines we've been taught.

These ancient truths ripple far beyond our planet. I believe intelligent life has always existed across the stars. And yet, the so-called great minds of today insist it's not possible. They cite distances measured in light years, the impossibility of faster-than-light travel, and various mathematical laws, I might remind you, that we ourselves invented. Time. Math. Space. All human constructs. Our attempts to explain the unexplainable. In reality, time may not exist at all—not in the way we define it. Sunrise to sunrise may mean nothing to a life form that experiences existence as a single eternal moment. Perhaps other civilizations see time not as a river but as a field, or a circle, or something we can't yet imagine. They may have learned to navigate great distances through manipulation of vibration and light, bending space itself in ways that we cannot comprehend. And why can't we comprehend it? Because our minds—still so very young—haven't evolved to that level yet. We're still crawling, spiritually speaking.

There are even theories—ones I feel deep truth in—that we live among countless dimensions simultaneously. Most can't perceive them, but some of us feel them, like faint pressure or a flicker at the edge of consciousness. Our Earth, our civilization, all of humankind is merely an embryo in the grand cosmic womb. The deeper vibrational understandings—things we may have once known—have been buried in us, waiting to be remembered. Only a few can tune into that ancient frequency. Even the greatest thinkers and prophets—Edgar Cayce, the sleeping prophet, and others like him—have only scratched the surface of universal wisdom. When I ponder this, it humbles me. All our little daily stresses, our obsessions with careers, money, status—they dissolve like mist in the morning sun. They are shadows compared to the light of universal truth. Sometimes I wish I could just dissolve into that light fully. To stop resisting, to simply be, to vibrate in harmony with everything—always.

It's hard, though. Life pulls at us. The noise of society drowns out the symphony of the stars. We chase things that mean nothing. We worry ourselves so much over the trivial things in life. But maybe, just maybe, the animals, the trees, the winds and the oceans are ahead of us. They live by natural law. They don't doubt or overanalyze. They simply are. They vibrate, they live, they accept their role in the great unfolding. How magnificent would it be for us to return to that state—to be fully interconnected, one with the rhythm of the universe? Imagine what we could become. Imagine humanity breathing as one, in unity, in love. But the ego—that old gatekeeper—won't let us go easily. It demands control, explanations, certainty. It fears surrender. And yet, surrender is exactly what we need. To pull back the veil, to drop the armor, to release the grip of "knowing" and allow ourselves to be felt into awareness. I know—I'm just a piano tuner speaking philosophically. But this is who I am. It's not something I studied; it's something I live.

I question. I feel. I surrender. I'm deeply flawed, like everyone, but I try to listen to what's beyond the noise.

I'm not much different from you, truly. The only thing that might set me apart is my willingness to go inward and feel what others might dismiss. To sit with the strange, the unseen, the intangible—and welcome it. My thoughts? Some of them have lived in me since childhood, others have come through study, dreams, past life regressions, and the quiet whispers of intuition. I believe much of it was planted in me before this life even began. And I urge you, gently, to open your own mind just a little more. Step back. Breathe. Question what you've been taught. Entertain the possibility that everything you know could be reimagined. Even our most advanced knowledge—our weather systems, our climate predictions—are infantile when measured against the ancient rhythms of the Earth. Mother Earth doesn't need saving; she is not fragile. She is transformative. She has shifted, burned, frozen, flooded, healed, and renewed herself for eons. She will continue to do so, with or without us.

Our modern tech age, for all its marvels, is just a blink. Yes, we've come far—especially in the last fifty years, but I'm convinced some of that knowledge wasn't entirely our own. I believe we've had help. There are whispers of technologies shared, of encounters that seeded inspiration, of reverse-engineered wisdom from beyond. Think about it: in less than two centuries, we've gone from horses to smartphones. That leap is cosmic. What happens when we get ten thousand years of that kind of growth? Or a hundred thousand? We would become unrecognizable to ourselves. So, I challenge you— make a commitment to yourself. Take small steps. Let your heart be curious. Explore. Be brave enough to think higher, feel deeper. Let go of the need to be right and embrace the possibility that we are part of something truly extraordinary. Let's come together, not just as humans, but as conscious beings of vibration, capable of harmonizing with each other and with the galaxies that cradle us. This unity, this shared awareness, is the hidden thread connecting us all. Let's pull on that thread. Let's remember who we are.

I blinked, and suddenly I was rolling through my sixties. At sixty-seven, I chose to slow down—just two days a week of piano work now. But that was enough. It kept me grounded, kept my hands and soul tuned to the great song of the Earth. The tuning fork of the universe still rang through me. Raelene's father, Mac, passed at the astonishing age of ninety-seven. His long life didn't surprise us—he came from hardy stock—but still, his passing left a great emptiness. He was the grandfather every child deserves—steady, warm, full of wisdom.

I kept doing what I loved. Fishing, and taking trips with Gwen, especially to Hawaii—our sacred place. Frank and Jan, dear friends, had a home there that welcomed us like an embrace. There's something about Hawaii—its air, its light, its pulse. I felt like I existed in another realm while there, like the veil between worlds was thinner. We also shared beautiful moments with Tim and Mandy, horse people like Gwen. Horses had always been her passion, her joy. I understood. The way she connected with them reminded me of how I connected with vibration itself.

I also picked up woodworking again—an homage to my dad, Ed. The smell of sawdust, the grain of wood beneath my fingers—it was all memory, and meditation, and creation. I blended his craftsmanship with my own artistic spirit and created something new. I also finished my proudest musical work—an album of original, Celtic-influenced pieces that felt like echoes of a past life. My daughter Kira married, and so did my son Casey. Kira gave tuning a try, but life as a mother took her elsewhere. Casey, though, picked up the torch. With my guidance, he walked the path—piano tuning and finance, a beautiful balance of soul and logic.

And here I stand, older, not done yet, but feeling something rising—a road ahead still filled with wonder. My life has been blessed. And the music, the vibration, the truth—it's all still singing.

18

FALITE DHACHAIDH

Well, it was astounding that me, Mr. Will Campbell had made it all the way to my seventies. Life somehow just flew by me, and now I finally looked very old. The glimpse of my older self from my first past life regression with Laura was now staring back at me from the mirror. That vision from my twenties slowly unfolded before me and came true. At that point in my life, I also lost my two remaining birth sisters, Maggie and Julie. Sadly, both endured tremendous abuse and trauma during their younger years. Part of me was thankful that they could finally escape that and be at peace. I was still in great physical shape for my age, just like I was my whole life. Oddly, at this stage of my life, things felt unusually familiar to me. I knew it was me tapping into my previous lives. However, lurking deep down, I could sense that there was an uneasy darkness, like a distant storm slowly creeping towards me.

Gwen, unfortunately, became very ill again and had to go to the hospital. Each year, as she got older, it became harder for her to recover from the physical ailments that plagued her most of her life. This time was different for us. I had seen Gwen, over all the years, come back from near death many times. If she was a cat, she would have been a super cat, because she had long outlived nine lives for sure. I was reminded of when I met her, and she told me that she only had five years left in her. She had told me back then that even though she looked great on the outside, her insides were wrecked. Well, somehow, here we were together twenty-one years later. We had many discussions over time regarding what would happen if the worst were to happen to her. Tragically, despite Gwen's resilient, beautiful spirit, her weakened body could take no more. I stayed by her bedside at her final stages of life. I was fortunate enough to tell her how much I deeply loved her and was beyond grateful for her in my life. We were so blessed to have our eternal souls connected from long ago, until now and beyond. As I held her face in my hands one last time, I kissed her lips as she quietly parted this world. I was engulfed in crushing sadness under a torrential flood of tears. My love was gone, and a part of my soul died with her. I had experienced tremendous loss in my present and past lives, but nothing would compare to the emptiness that I felt. I went through the funeral services and gave a heartfelt speech in honor of her. No one knew it, but I had given that speech years before in my mind, like I did at so many other funerals. Gwen was cremated, according to her wishes. I kept a small bit of her ashes in a locket around my neck, close to my heart. The rest of her ashes I spread in Hawaii and Maine, our two favorite places. I struggled greatly to move forward without her, but I was thankful that she didn't have to suffer any longer. I was also able to take comfort in our eternal vibrational connection that we both truly understood.

Through the rest of my seventies, I focused most on my family; nothing could be more important in my life. My daughter Kira was blessed with two children, a boy named Liam Will and a girl named Cara Rae. Also, my son Casey too was blessed with two children, a boy, Jackson Smith, and a girl, Fiona Patricia. My heart just bursts with tremendous joy over having all my beautiful grandchildren in my life. That was what life was truly all about; a wonderful legacy and the opportunity to pass on my knowledge and love with all my beautiful grandchildren. I was having tons of fun as their proud Pop Pop every chance I had.

I continued to do some piano tuning one or two days a week, depending on how I felt, but it was very limited. Over the years, I was very fortunate to meet and work for so many incredible people, and a lot of famous, talented musicians as well. My woodworking business had taken off quite a bit because there was nothing else like the things that I was building; they were uniquely my own creations. I went fishing every chance I could, and it was always a bonus to have my son or daughters and grandchildren fishing by my side. I was so happy to see them out in the beauties of nature and vibrationally connected to the Earth and Universe. Every once in a great while, Neil would reach out to me and coax me into giving another lecture. It always felt wonderful to share my thoughts and ideas with new beautiful people, but I was getting tired. Incredibly, the old vessel that my soul resided in remarkably made it to seventy-nine years old. I found myself not being able to walk quite as far, because I would often quickly lose my breath.

One day I was out fishing with my son Casey, and I was in a beautiful happy place near the water as usual. I noticed my friend, the old beaver, constantly swimming near me. I had known that family of beavers for many years, but something was different this time. The big male beaver kept swimming up close to me repeatedly. It was as if the beaver was staring right into my soul. Suddenly, I clutched my chest, and I struggled to breathe. My son Casey panicked but remained calm enough to call 911 for help. The ambulance came quickly as I was passing out. The next thing I knew, I was in a hospital bed surrounded by my beloved family. I could feel the energy in the room, and it was full of concern and sadness. I was extremely weak, and my breathing was very shallow. I was still quite coherent, and I was very much aware why everyone was with me. The doctor came in and said, "Mr. Campbell, I'm Doctor Kordian, chief cardiologist here at Sacred Heart Medical Center. Will, you have suffered a substantial heart attack, and you are lucky to be alive. Unfortunately, the damage to your heart was very severe. If you were a stronger, younger man, we might consider a heart transplant for you. However, at your age, we would not recommend that, and you would not survive the procedure. For now, we want to just make you as comfortable as possible. There is no definite timeframe, but you most likely have just a few days left. If there is anything you or your family needs, our staff is here for you." In a low, weak voice, I thanked Dr. Kordian. I could see how upset everyone was, and I did my best to put off calming vibrational energy to all of them. I was too weak to go home, and I would never want to put that burden on my family anyway. I quietly said, well, maybe someone could bring in a little goldfish bowl and a small fishing pole for me; maybe I could at least check out while fishing. They all laughed because they knew it was my favorite pastime, but I knew this was very painful for everyone. With a tear in his eye, my son

Casey said, "Dad, you know you'll be eighty years old in two days." I whispered, "The old Scorpio will certainly try to make it." My family knew my wishes were to be cremated. Just like my past lives with the Algonquins and my ancient Celtic tribe, my soul would be released and moved on through fire. I was grateful for the opportunity to speak individually with all my children. I first let them know how deeply I loved them all. I told them how special each one of them was to me and how they have their own unique purpose in life to fulfill now. I told all my children that it was very important to me that they pass on all the knowledge and love that I had given to them to my grandchildren. I also told them that even though they would be sad, it was understandable in a time like this, but I also wanted everyone to celebrate my life and all that I had shared with them. I reassured them that I was blessed with a wonderful life and that there was no greater gift than my children, grandchildren, family, and friends throughout my life. They would all be OK, and they all must move forward on their own unique journeys. I told them that I too am moving forward to another place, and my soul was at peace with that.

For me, the time in the hospital seemed a bit endless. I continued to weaken, and I was less and less awake. My family continued the vigil with me and rotated in and out around the clock. My son took the lead for the family and stayed in constant contact with the medical staff as the end became nearer. Finally, after two days of me hanging on, I had reached my eightieth birthday. On November 5, 2043, with my family surrounding me, I slowly closed my eyes forever. As I took one last breath, I left my physical body, the vessel that my soul resided in for this lifetime.

The medical staff pronounced my death at 4 AM. With that, Mr. Will Campbell departed our beautiful Mother Earth forever.

I could feel my real self, which was my soul, leaving my body. I was able to reflect on all my past journeys as well, and I felt complete and happy. Unlike my previous life passings, this time I did not worry if I had done enough for those that I loved. I by no means led a perfect life, but I felt that I was able to learn from my poor choices at every fork on my journey's road. I had also broken the vicious circle of abuse that haunted my birth family. I passed on my knowledge and love from all my lives to my children and grandchildren and many others. I was completely content and ready to fully pass on. Just like the light at my birth, I peacefully and eagerly moved towards it. Gwen was lovingly smiling right beside me. Then I was joyfully greeted by my foster parents, Ed and Mary, along with Liz, my foster sister. Polly, Raelene's mother, was also happy and beside me. My older siblings, Lona, Jack, Maggie, Jimmy, and Julie surrounded me with all their love as well. My soul was filled with so much love—it was beautiful. As I moved deeper towards the light, I reached another level, just as Vince the time traveler had told me. There I was greeted by Mohegan, my Algonquin father, along with Aiyana, my Algonquin wife. It was so beautifully comforting. Then, a little deeper still, I was met by Brennus, my Celtic father, and Eilidh, my Celtic wife from Skara Brae. Their energy was magical as they guided me forward closer to the light. I then began to see a distant glowing mist swirling in front of me. As my soul approached the mist, it became incredibly bright and surreal. Finally, I slowly drifted through the mist and entered the most enchanting, beautiful world. Standing before me were the glowing ones that I knew from long ago. Once again, my eternal fate would be judged by the ancient elders.

They were Belleek and Dagda, my protectors, along with Brigid, my teacher of wisdom and healing, who were right alongside me. Also, Mercury, my guide of messaging and time travel, and Ecne, my mentor of enlightenment, all surrounded me. The elders then joined with my soul, which was a unification of all the layers of my conscious self. Finally, with one collective voice through thought, in vibrational unison, they said to me:

Leith, fáilte dhachaigh, the ancient Scottish words for,

Welcome home.